D1375244

# Will I be fat in heaven?

### & other curious questions

Copyright © 2021 J.John

Published in 2021 by Philo Trust
Witton House, Lower Road, Chorleywood, Rickmansworth, WD3 5LB
www.canonjjohn.com

The right of J.John to be identified as the author of this work has been asserted
by him in accordance with the Copyright, Designs and Patents Act 1988.

All rights reserved. No part of this publication may be reproduced or transmitted
in any form or by any means without permission in writing from the publisher.

ISBN: 978-1-912326-21-1

Unless otherwise marked, Scripture quotations are taken from The Holy Bible,
New International Version (Anglicised edition), copyright © 1979, 1984, 2011 Biblica.
Used by permission of Hodder & Stoughton Publishers, an Hachette UK company.
All rights reserved.

Scripture quotations marked 'KJV' are from The Authorised (King James) Version.
Rights in the Authorised Version in the United Kingdom are vested in the Crown.
Reproduced by permission of the Crown's patentee, Cambridge University Press.

Illustrated by Tom Tinn-Disbury, t.tinn.disbury@gmail.com
www.tomtinndisbury.com

Print Management by Verité CM Ltd
www.veritecm.com

Printed in the UK

# Will I be fat in heaven?

## & other curious questions

## J.JOHN

### ILLUSTRATED BY TOM TINN-DISBURY

# CONTENTS

PART THREE:

# QUESTIONS ABOUT GOD, GOOD AND EVIL

PART FOUR:

# BEING MADE RIGHT WITH GOD

# ABOUT QUESTIONS

A couple of years ago I produced a little book called *That's a Good Question!* which tackled thirty-two questions asked by children, some of them rather unusual, including such things as 'Will my dog go to heaven?' and 'Why do people die before they are old?' As I wrote the answers, I came to realise that, despite the simple language used by the children, what they were raising were deep and serious matters. Indeed, I recognised many of the questions as being those that, phrased more elegantly, I often get from adults.

In thinking about who asks these questions I realise they come from both those 'within the faith' and those outside it. Sometimes I get them from Christians who have been struck by something they have read or heard and want to know 'what the answer is'. Sometimes these questions come from those who are not yet believers but who are thinking about Christianity. Sometimes Christians who are sharing their faith have had questions posed to them. Bearing in mind these different sources of questions, I've tried here to address as wide an audience as possible. I've done my best to take nothing for granted, although I have assumed that any reader has access to a Bible and isn't thrown by me quoting Bible references such as Ephesians 6:17.

So recognising the importance of questions, and after much thought and discussion with friends, I sat down and came up with a list of thirty-eight questions that adults might ask. In reality, I could easily have doubled that number. You will find here serious questions but also one or two that appear frivolous such as 'Will I be fat in heaven?' Actually, that turns out to be a question which raises some very interesting issues about who we are and what we will be.

Although these are questions adults ask, I've tried to keep the responses as simple as possible and hope they will also be accessible to younger people.

Finally, in terms of how to read these questions I suggest you think about them in terms of you and I sitting down in comfortable chairs in some quiet coffee shop and chatting together. Don't read them all at once – take time to drink your coffee or tea and think about the responses.

# SHOULD WE ASK QUESTIONS?

The topic of questions raises questions. Should those people who are either Christians or who are enquiring about Christianity ask questions? Let me suggest four situations in which questions can and should be asked.

FIRST, questions can be to do with the *confirmation* of the faith. If you've ever listened to anybody who was caught up in a financial swindle you will probably have heard them say something like: 'We were told that we mustn't ask questions.' There are reasons for this: one way of finding out whether something is really true is to ask probing questions. So, if you watch a realistic crime drama you will know that it's the responsibility of any detective to ask questions of the suspect in order to test an alibi. ('You say you were at the cinema on Tuesday night? So, what was the film?') A similar procedure works in science: someone proposes a theory and then other tests and experiments are carried out to see whether it really works. If your hard questions are met with satisfactory answers, then that's a very strong indication that you're dealing with something that is true.

**SECOND**, questions can be to do with the *foundation* of our faith. So, imagine someone who has just become a Christian by putting their faith in Jesus. Immediately, they are full of questions, many of which contain the word *now*. What am I supposed to believe now about this subject? How do I behave now? How do I pray now? What's the best way to read the Bible now? These are important questions and, in my experience, it's absolutely vital that they are answered well. In order for buildings to endure, they need good foundations: so do we.

**THIRD**, questions can be to do with the *exploration* of our faith. In this case asking questions is rather like going into the attic of the house you have just bought and shining a torch around to see what is there. Questions are a way of developing and enlarging what we know. So, for instance, imagine a young person who, having grown up in a comfortable and secure Christian environment, now finds themselves at university facing all sorts of new and sometimes disturbing ideas. Inevitably, they want to know what their faith has to say about these things and how it should be applied.

**FOURTH**, questions can be to do with the *declaration* of our faith. Anyone with a living Christian faith should be constantly trying to engage with those around them who don't know about Jesus. They may want to speak out, either to defend Christianity against criticism or to share the good news about Jesus with those who do not know him. If you were planning to buy a new car you would want to ask lots of questions and look carefully at it before making any sort of commitment. Anybody considering a faith that they know will change their life would, I hope, be no less questioning. So if you've been a Christian for some time you may look at some of these question titles and say, 'Oh, that's not a problem for me.' Fair enough, but it may be a problem for someone you meet.

So whether for confirmation, foundation, exploration or declaration, questions are good. We shouldn't be afraid of asking questions or trying to answer them. So, let's get started!

# PART ONE

# QUESTIONS ABOUT THE BIBLE

In most of the answers that follow you will find that I refer to the Bible. Christianity centres on the belief that in the pages of the Bible we read what God wants to say to the human race. It follows from this that the Bible should form the basis on which we decide what we believe and how we should live. Although some Christians might argue that reason or church tradition are also important, it is accepted that the authority for what we believe is God's written Word, the Bible.

Nevertheless, the decision to take the Bible as being our authority raises questions and it makes sense to deal with these at the start.

# HOW CAN THE BIBLE BE INSPIRED BY GOD WHEN THERE ARE DIFFERENT VERSIONS?

Christians often refer to the Bible as the 'Word of God' and talk about it as being 'inspired' or 'God-breathed'. This is a claim that the Bible is not just the product of human beings but one whose writing was guided or supervised by God's Holy Spirit.

That claim goes back to the Bible itself (see, for example, Isaiah 55:11; 1 Thessalonians 2:13; Ephesians 6:17; 2 Timothy 3:16; Hebrews 4:12). Such a claim, however, raises many questions. Let me give you one example: how can all the many Bible versions in various languages be 'God's Word'? Indeed, there are fifty Bible versions in English alone. Are they *all* 'inspired'?

Let's step back for a moment. An idea that I will be frequently referring to in these answers is that God is 'outside our universe'. Let me give two illustrations about what I mean here. One is that we are like fish in a small pond; the other is that we are like invented creatures within some vast and extraordinarily complex computer simulation. In neither case

15

can we have any real idea of what lies beyond or outside the universe in which we find ourselves and we certainly could not investigate it. If that sort of situation applies to the universe in which we live – and Christians have always said that something like it must apply – you will realise the only way we can know about God is if he tells us something about who he is and what he expects from us.

I think we can best understand the idea of the Bible as being inspired as a process that involves five stages.

FIRST, God created individuals such as Isaiah, Matthew and Paul with their own distinct personalities and backgrounds and then worked with them through his Spirit so that what they wrote was exactly what he wanted them to say (2 Peter 1:20–21). Importantly, that's quite different from God dictating something through a person whether they liked it or not. For example, the different gospels reflect the different personalities of their authors and Paul's letters differ from John's.

SECOND, the same Holy Spirit then encouraged and guided those who received these messages, whether letters, prophecies or historical accounts, to treat them as coming from God. As a result, they were kept safe from destruction or alteration.

THIRD, the Holy Spirit, again working in collaboration with God's people, ensured that these messages were faithfully copied and preserved safely over several centuries.

(This isn't too hard to believe: all the evidence we have is that those people who copied what they believed to be holy documents were incredibly careful not to allow mistakes.) The result of this is that we can be reasonably certain that the Greek and Hebrew manuscripts which form the basis of our Bibles are what the original writers actually wrote.

FOURTH, the work of God's Holy Spirit has continued to the present day in helping faithful believers to translate God's Word from the original languages into the thousands of different languages that people speak today.

FIFTH, and finally, the involvement of the Spirit in the Bible does not stop there but continues to the point when you and I read the Bible today. If we read it prayerfully, God's Spirit will speak through it to us.

The result of these different workings of the Spirit is what we have in the Bible: a book that is 'divine' because it comes from God but also human because it was written, preserved and translated through men and women. This view of the Bible as being divine and human is both encouraging and challenging.

It's *encouraging* because it tells us that God didn't simply announce a message thousands of years ago and leave it to get lost, distorted, misunderstood or simply forgotten by human beings. Through his Spirit, God himself has been continuously involved in the creation, preservation and translation of the Bible. Precisely because of the working of the Holy Spirit we can expect God to speak to us today.

The *challenge* is that both translators and readers need to work to allow God to speak clearly through his Word. Translators need to master the ancient languages, examine the manuscripts and think hard about how to render the original language of the Bible documents into a translation that will speak clearly to people today. We who are readers need to get hold of the best Bible translation we can and read it with reverence and obedience and – this is important – with the expectation that God will speak to us.

Let me offer a final thought. The most important thing about the Bible is that it reveals Jesus Christ and extends an invitation for everyone to come to know him. Jesus is, after all, the one who is the Word made flesh (John 1:14) and the one who saves us. That's a very important point: we are not to worship the Bible but the one who it talks about. It's a vital difference that we mustn't overlook. It's a little bit like being invited to meet someone important at their home. When you knock on the door and they come out to welcome you, to ignore them but stand there admiring the doorframe is to completely miss the point. God has spoken to us through his Spirit in the Bible: let's listen to him.

# WHY DO WE BELIEVE
# THE BIBLE IS TRUE?

The fact that I frequently refer to the Bible here raises its own question: why do we believe the Bible is true? Let me give you one inadequate reason and four good ones.

The inadequate reason to believe the Bible is true is simply because it claims that it is inspired by God (as, for example, in Psalm 119:160; 2 Timothy 3:16). The problem is the obvious one: just because something claims that it is true doesn't mean that it really *is* true. There are lots of books about God, heaven and everything else that claim to be true but are actually imaginary. So let's note the claim to be true that the Bible makes for itself, but put it to one side and look at four other reasons.

**THE FIRST REASON** to believe that the Bible is true is because it is a book that is set in the real world of history and geography. Where we know something relevant from archaeology or history, it either supports the Bible's account or casts new light upon it. This accuracy encourages us to believe that the documents that make up the Bible are reliable records of events and have been passed on carefully from generation to generation to us.[1]

---

[1] I've discussed the very strong evidence for the reliability of the gospels with Chris Walley in the book *Jesus Christ – The Truth* published by Philo.

**THE SECOND REASON** is that, throughout the Bible, we read a single story: the rescue of the human race. The first pages of the Bible tell us of how, in the distant past, God made the universe, and its final pages mirror this by telling how, in the future, God will remake the universe. In between we read how human beings rebelled against God and how, over many centuries, he gradually brought them back to himself, finally coming to earth in the person of Jesus to make everything right. The fact that the Bible has a single common theme from beginning to end would be understandable if it was a book written by a single author. But it isn't. The extraordinary fact is that it is actually a collection of 'little books' written by many different people from different countries speaking different languages over a period of at least 1,600 years. Yet despite these differences we have this single plotline. The only way I can explain this is that behind these very different human authors, God himself was prompting and guiding what was to be written.

**THE THIRD REASON** for believing the Bible is true is the way that it takes a single viewpoint. Despite all these different authors writing over many centuries and from different cultures, the books of the Bible are in agreement with each other. So, from the beginning to the very end of the Bible, we read that God is just one, that he is eternal and all-powerful and that we should think of him as being both a loving parent and a firm judge. We also get a common picture of the human race; although we are made in God's image and are gifted with intelligence and wisdom, we are deeply flawed and have all chosen to rebel against God. This single viewpoint is also seen in the way that, from the first page to the last, the Bible tells us of God's loving care, his extraordinary patience and his willingness to pay the highest price to defeat evil and to create a new and more faithful people of God. Again, this extraordinary harmony across a variety of writers, separated by cultures and centuries, suggests that God himself was behind the writing of the Bible.

THE FINAL REASON for believing the Bible is true is the way that Jesus remains the centre of the whole story of the Bible. In the Old Testament we read prophecies of a coming King (or *Messiah*) who will fulfil God's promises; in the New Testament we read of what Jesus did as the Messiah on earth and what he is doing now as King in heaven; in both Old and New Testaments we read of what he will do in the future. Ultimately, Jesus himself claimed to be the focus of God's Word (John 5:39) but at the same time he clearly viewed the Bible (which for him, of course, was our 'Old Testament') as reliable and trustworthy (Matthew 26:53–56; Luke 24:25–27; John 5:39–47). And if it's good enough for Jesus, it's good enough for me.

FINALLY, let me give you my own personal experience. I have trusted the Bible for forty-five years, I have made its truth the foundation of all that I do, and I have shared from it to hundreds of thousands of people. It has never let me down. I don't think it will let you down either.

# IS THE BIBLE LITERALLY TRUE?

Questions breed questions and this is one that arises from the previous one about believing that the Bible is true.

'Ah yes,' I can hear someone say, 'but is it *literally* true?' It's a common enough question but it's actually rather messy. Is it asking whether every single phrase found in the Bible is to be understood as the sort of straightforward statement of fact such as 'London is the capital of the United Kingdom'? I doubt whether any Christian really reads the Bible like that.

To do so would mean you believed that, in reality, God was a rock (Psalm 62:2) and that he had nostrils (Psalm 18:15) and that Jesus was both a door and a vine (John 10:9; 15:1). The fact is that all languages use images or word pictures. So, for instance, in English we talk about being 'over the moon', it's 'raining cats and dogs', having 'to bite the bullet' and something costing 'an arm and a leg' and we never take them literally.

Given that the Bible was written in an age before science and in a world a long way removed from ours, it's inevitable that we can sometimes struggle to work out whether what we read is a factual statement to be taken at face value or an image or symbol.

So if in a modern book we were to come across the expression 'the ends of the earth', we would know it was not meant to be understood literally, but how would we interpret it in a book written thousands of years ago? We would have to make a decision as to whether the author meant it literally or not. In the case of the Bible, it's not helped because none of its languages have the quotation marks that writers use today to indicate they are using imagery or quoting from some other source. Actually, to imagine that every statement in the Bible must be factually and 'literally' true is to deny it is not just God's inspired and reliable Word but also a very varied and very human book. Within the Bible's pages are history, poetry, preaching, proverbs and visions, and each of them uses language in a different way.

So how are we to decide what is to be interpreted as factually true and what is to be interpreted as merely an image or a symbol? The rule of interpretation we use is simple in theory but hard to apply in practice: it's that we do what we would do with any modern piece of writing and interpret what we read in the *sense that the writer intended.* If we convince ourselves that he or she meant us to understand something as real and factually true, then that's how we accept it. If, on the other hand, we are confident that what we have is the language of imagery or poetry, then we don't interpret it literally. In fact, for most of the books of the Bible, there are few problems: the book of Psalms is poetry, the gospels are clearly history, the visionary book of Revelation overflows with symbolic language. Yes, there are areas of difficulty; for example, what type of language is being used in the first chapter of Genesis? How are we to treat the large numbers used in some of the Old Testament books such as Joshua and 1 and 2 Samuel? How factual are the descriptions of paradise in the last chapters of the book of Revelation? On these matters Christians disagree. Yet – and this is a really important point – on the big central issues of the faith there is no dispute.

I think that when it comes to how we view the Bible we need to walk midway between two extreme and equally wrong positions. One extreme is to find truth where there is only symbol. For example, I have heard people defending the idea of a flat earth on the basis of the Bible talking about the 'four corners of the earth' (Isaiah 11:12 KJV).

The other wrong extreme occurs where people try to get around the clear truths of the Bible by declaring them as 'nothing more than images'. For instance, you can find statements that say things like, 'Of course, Jesus didn't really rise from the dead; it's just some sort of symbol for hope.' In fact, the gospels and the letters of the New Testament clearly state that the resurrection was an absolute reality; after all, the risen Jesus could eat food and be touched (Luke 24:42; John 20:24–28).

We must make allowances for the personalities of the writers of the individual books of the Bible, we must accept that methods of reporting events were not done then as we would do them today and we must accept that, in places, we may not have fully understood the meaning of the original text.

Yet to accept these limitations in no way obscures the fact that the central message of the Bible is remarkably clear. It is a statement that, in Jesus, God paid the price for our wrongdoing through his death, but a statement that comes with a condition: to accept that forgiveness we must accept Jesus as Saviour and Lord. Ultimately, the big challenge that we all meet when we look at the Bible is not how to interpret a few specific passages but deciding whether we are going to accept or reject the offer God has set before us.

# WHAT ABOUT ALL THE BLOODSHED THAT SEEMS TO BE COMMANDED BY GOD IN THE OLD TESTAMENT?

This question focuses on those passages in the Old Testament where God commands – or seems to command – the killing of people, whether in legal punishment or in battle. It's not just the spilt blood that people are troubled by. It's the fact that they see an inconsistency between orders in the Old Testament that seem to say 'kill your enemies' and the clear New Testament teaching of 'love your enemies'.

There's no point in denying that the Old Testament has a number of difficult passages involving God and death. We read of a number of crimes for which God said there was to be a death penalty; these include murder, idolatry, breaking the Sabbath and adultery (for example, Genesis 9:6; Deuteronomy 13:6–10; Numbers 15:32–36; Leviticus 20:10). Perhaps the best way of looking at these is to see them as God making the point, in the toughest of ages, that he and his rules were to be taken seriously. In reality, we don't know how often the death penalty was actually imposed. It's interesting that when in the New Testament Jesus was asked to approve a stoning for adultery, he found a wise way of making it impossible to carry out (John 8:1–11).

The most difficult case involving bloodshed is where God orders his people, Israel, to forcibly destroy the Canaanites who were occupying the 'promised land' and to take their property in a 'holy war' that seems to have involved the slaughter of whole communities (for example, Deuteronomy 7:1–2; Joshua 6:21; 8:24–26). Let me make a number of points.

- We are talking about a period over 3,000 years ago and these were warlike and brutal times in that part of the world. Confrontations were merciless and when nations (not just Israel) conquered other people, slaughter was 'just the way things were'. That doesn't make it right, but it puts it in context.

- God's commands to Israel were about a specific task for a specific place: the taking of the 'promised land'. They were given for a specific time too; in fact, most of these 'holy war' incidents occurred within a single generation. Nothing similar is recorded in the later books of the Old Testament and there is nothing remotely like this in the New Testament, although some of the symbolic language in the book of Revelation is warlike.

- Some of the reports may have involved dramatic exaggeration, a bit like today when you say that your football team 'annihilated the opposition'. Of course not literally!

- The Canaanites were not innocent. They are described as worshipping evil gods and committing atrocities, including child sacrifice (Leviticus 18:21–28; Deuteronomy 9:5, 12:29–31). In fact, we are told that God gave the Canaanites 400 years to repent; an opportunity they ignored (Genesis 15:13–16). So, these troubling commands were God judging the Canaanites. (Significantly, in due course, when God's people started committing the same sins, they were judged in a similar way.)

- We mustn't lose sight of God's overall purpose. The big picture of the Bible is of God creating through his people, Israel, a way in which the Messiah – Jesus – could come to save the world. For that to happen, he needed people who were utterly devoted to him, something that was rather difficult because the Israelites tended to adopt the very worst beliefs and traditions from those they lived amongst. To create a situation in which Jesus could come meant that the Canaanites and their beliefs and practices had to be totally removed (Deuteronomy 7:3–5; 12:2–3). It's like a surgeon cutting away diseased tissue in order to ensure long-term healing or a farmer removing weeds before planting a new crop.

Perhaps above all, we need to remember that these tough commands were given for a long-gone situation that is not relevant today. There are now no Canaanites and while the followers of Jesus can be considered to be a 'holy people', their 'promised land' is in heaven. Despite what misguided people say, there are no 'holy wars' to be fought in the twenty-first century.

It's worth noting that at the time of Jesus, many Jewish people thought that, with their 'promised land' ruled by the brutal and idolatrous Romans, it was time to bring back this concept of holy war. Despite this, Jesus rejected any idea of violence towards Roman rule. Jesus told his followers that if Roman soldiers ordered them to carry a burden, they should offer to carry it twice the distance demanded (Matthew 5:38–42).

And finally, it's easy for us to judge people in the ancient past and say how nasty and horrible they were. But are we really so very much better? We possess bombs that can wipe out entire cities, run economic policies that allow nations to starve, and have such an appetite for 'things' that we seem to have damaged the world's climates, devastated its wildlife and polluted its sea and air. Perhaps we should be a little more cautious about where we point the finger. To borrow a phrase Jesus used when challenged over the death penalty: 'let him who is without sin cast the first stone' (see John 8:7).

# WHY, IF THE BIBLE IS THE INSPIRED WORD OF GOD, IS THE SCIENCE IN IT NOT MORE ACCURATE?

Some critics of the Bible make a great deal of the fact that it is not as scientifically accurate as they would like. So, for instance, they protest that the story of creation doesn't fit with geology; the references to the sun, moon or stars don't fit with astronomy. The argument goes that, as these are wrong, the Bible cannot be inspired by a God who not only knows about everything, but actually made everything.

So why isn't the Bible better when it touches on science? It's a fascinating question and let me offer some thoughts in response.

**FIRST OF ALL**, this is a question that seems to me to misunderstand the nature of the Bible. As I pointed out earlier, the Bible neither descended miraculously from heaven nor was it dictated through individuals who were no more than God's mouthpiece. Because the documents of the Bible are not just divine but also human, God spoke through individuals using their language and ideas. That means that it uses the concepts of the authors' time and culture, even if we now view them as being naïve or simplistic. One of the great principles that runs through the Bible from beginning to end is that God respects who human beings are. A result of this is that, in matters of science, God doesn't change or correct the scientific knowledge of the time.

If you think about it, imagining that God might have produced a Bible more in tune with modern science poses real practical problems. Take for instance Exodus 16:21 where the author – traditionally Moses – writes about when the sun grew hot. To make this scientifically accurate the Holy Spirit would have had to explain to Moses that the sun was in fact a large sphere of gas at a very high temperature at an enormous distance away which, due to the rotation of the earth, was now directly overhead at noon so that the rays of sunlight hit the ground directly, rather going through the atmosphere at an angle.

At this point you can imagine Moses furrowing his brow and muttering, 'Excuse me, Lord, can you explain the words *sphere, gas, temperature, rotation, rays* and *angle?*' There were not even the basic concepts for discussing science 3,500 years ago. Indeed, if Moses had used the language of modern science, he would have utterly failed in what he was supposed to do: communicate God's truth to his contemporaries.

THERE'S MORE. Let's suppose God had given a science education to the ancient Israelites. Armed with physics, chemistry and mathematics his people would have become more technologically advanced than their neighbours and soon become a military superpower with steel swords and armour-plated chariots. It may sound wonderful, but the reality is that God's people seem to stay closest to God when they are weakest; it's an idea that the New Testament develops in 1 Corinthians 1:18–31. It's an interesting fact that Israelites were actually less scientifically advanced than some of their neighbours; the Philistines in particular seem to have had the technological edge over them (1 Samuel 13:19–23). Here, weakness is strength.

Behind this question is an attitude that treats science far more seriously than it should. Don't get me wrong, I'm not anti-science: I've had my life saved by antibiotics, I enjoy using the Internet, I fly on planes and I enjoy David Attenborough programmes. But there is a naïve form of thinking that puts scientific knowledge above everything else. The fact is that, from a very important point of view, all science information is trivia. Yes, you read that right: *trivia*. You see, science does not say anything meaningful about the really big questions of life: What is love? What is the purpose of life? What happens to us after death? Why not cheat, lie or kill? Does *anything* really matter? I could multiply these questions endlessly and not a single one of them is answered by science.

NOT ONLY THAT, I find an arrogance in this question. It's the assumption that the Bible should address the issues of twenty-first-century human beings who are focused on technology almost to the point of obsession and idolatry. Actually, the Bible is for all cultures at all times and has been read and understood by Roman slaves and rocket scientists. Linked with this narrow perspective is the wonderfully naïve assumption that modern science is actually correct. It's a sobering thought that if, seventy years ago, you were to have written the history of the universe in a hundred words, it would today be something of great amusement. Who knows what revisions tomorrow's science will make of today's theories?

FINALLY, although the Bible does not give answers in terms of modern science, it does something more important: it provides a framework in which science can exist. Throughout the Bible what we are shown are men and women standing alone before God in a natural world which obeys laws that they have to respect and obey. It's no accident that modern science grew out of Christianity: the Bible provides a cultural soil, freed from the choking weeds of superstition, in which the plant of science can grow well and free. So if you're looking for the Bible to be a science textbook, well, I'm sorry you're going to be disappointed. Yet very few things – if any – in human culture have had such a positive influence on science as the Bible.

# WHY DO THERE SEEM TO BE CONTRADICTIONS IN THE BIBLE?

Contradictions are important. Take, for instance, a criminal investigation: although it might be hard to prove that what a witness says is true, if it can be shown that there are contradictions in what they say, that is very strong evidence that it's false. So the claims of contradictions in the Bible should be treated seriously.

Certainly, what I'd prefer to call 'claimed' or 'apparent' contradictions do occur. So, both 1 Samuel 31:1–6 and 2 Samuel 1:4–10 tell of how King Saul died in battle yet there are strong differences in the accounts. Did Jesus heal one blind man in Jericho (Mark 10:46; Luke 18:35) or two (Matthew 20:30)? There are many other cases. Many critics of Christianity have claimed that such apparent contradictions are sufficient to demonstrate that the Bible cannot be inspired by God. This raises a number of complex issues but let me offer a few comments that may be helpful.

In this area of 'contradictions' there are two basic kinds. One is the claim that there are specific instances where, when you compare different books of the Bible, there seem to be factual contradictions to do with names, numbers and events.

The other – far more serious – is the claim that there are theological contradictions within the Bible, most notoriously if you compare what the Old and New Testaments say about the character of God.

Generally speaking, it's helpful to remember that much of the problem here comes from a mistaken view of the Bible. You see, if you believe that the Bible was dictated by God to a single author at a single time in a single language then *any* contradiction would be an obvious problem. Yet as I've pointed out earlier, the Christian understanding is that what we have in our Bibles is a series of documents from different individuals who had differing personalities and perspectives. We might express it like this: God didn't dictate John's gospel; instead, he created the John who wrote it. The inevitable result of this is that John's gospel reflects John's educational background, outlook, culture and spiritual experience. And as John was not Matthew, Mark or Luke, so a very different outlook on events is in fact what you would expect.

With that in mind let me make some specific responses about any so-called contradictions.

- We need to accept that ancient writers had different standards of writing than we have today. For example, they seem to have been happier with omitting details or simplifying a story than we would be. It's ironic that at a time when we would never criticise an African writer for writing in an African way, we find it easy to criticise ancient literature and its authors for not maintaining our modern western expectations.

- There are issues of translation. Sometimes we may have misunderstood the precise sense of the Hebrew or the Greek. Mind you, if you compare something like the Authorised (King James) Version of the Bible published in 1611 with a modern Bible you will find that despite 400 years of scholarship, the main difference lies in the fact that the English used has been updated to allow the Bible to communicate more effectively to a modern audience. There are only a very few changes in meaning.

- Although Christians believe the Bible text is trustworthy, we don't have the original manuscripts and so it is possible that minor copying errors may well have crept in. (That's why scholars and translators constantly seek out the best and oldest manuscripts.) Again, despite the discovery of many new manuscripts, there have been few, if any, changes made over the last 500 years, and very few of any real significance.

- Sometimes what we have in the Bible is a difference of perspective. One writer sees events from one viewpoint, the other from another. Here it's worth remembering that when we view an object with two eyes, each eye sends the brain a slightly different image. Far from these two different images being contradictory, taken together they allow us to get a three-dimensional picture.

- It's worth remembering that life is sufficiently complex that, if you want to be critical, you can find contradictions in almost everything. Ask a husband and wife to write down what they did during the week and you will no doubt find differences in those accounts which, if you wanted to be critical, you could claim were contradictions.

- Let me remind you that the contradictions are claimed, not proven. Take the two instances given earlier. The second account of Saul's death may be what the witness invented and, in the Jericho instance, Mark and Luke may simply have chosen to select just one of the two blind men who were healed.

What about the more serious charge that there is a theological contradiction in how God appears between the Old and New Testaments? In fact, the idea that God is stern and judgemental in the Old Testament and loving and forgiving in the New Testament is a careless caricature. It overlooks the reality that not only is God often described as gracious in the Old Testament but that the idea of judgement is not absent in the New Testament. What can be said is that there is a progression and development of theology through the Bible. It is like looking down from a mountain top on some unknown landscape as the sun gradually rises. At first you see only the main features but as the sunlight brightens you begin to see far more and to understand how everything fits together. So, with the coming of Christ, the picture of who God is becomes illuminated so that we can see everything in a deeper, fuller and richer way. In one sense nothing has changed; in another everything has.

Finally, let me turn the argument around. In the Bible we have books from forty authors, from very different cultures, written in three languages over a period of sixteen centuries. What is truly remarkable is not the contradictions but the consistency: it is the same story from beginning to end.

# PART TWO

# QUESTIONS ABOUT GOD

The great starting point for how we live our lives is God. If he exists, then how we think about everything and live every part of our life is extraordinarily altered. The meaning and purpose of the world, what we do and say, are all fundamentally changed. Yet to seriously think about a God who doesn't just make the universe but keeps it going, a God who simultaneously manages stars and yet knows our every thought, is to invite questions. Here are just a few.

# HOW DO WE KNOW ABOUT GOD?

This is a vital question. Human beings can speculate about God endlessly and can make up ideas about him (or *her* or *it*) but there is a problem. Any God seriously worth considering – and certainly the God of Christianity – has got to be phenomenally greater than we can imagine. He is the one who has made the universe and keeps everything in it going from stars to snails, galaxies to goldfish. All that happens is under his control: as the phrase goes 'history is *his* story'. Utterly invisible to us, undetectable by any scientific instrument, God sees everything, knows everything and oversees everything that happens.

So how can we know about God? The teaching in the Jewish faith and the Christianity that builds on it has always been that by ourselves we can know very little, if anything, about God. We are like actors in a play trying to say something sensible about the author of the script which we are following. Yet Christian teaching says that the situation is not hopeless because God has chosen to make himself known to us. That process of God revealing himself – what is sometimes called 'revelation' – comes in three forms: through nature, through the Bible and through Jesus Christ.

**THE FIRST WAY** God speaks to us is in nature. Although people may differ in what they feel the natural world says to them, it seems to be a very common experience for someone to walk in a vast forest, see the enormity of the ocean or gaze up at the grandeur of the starlit night sky and become aware of 'something' or even a 'someone' behind it all. In fact, many individuals feel that they are in some way in the presence of God and sense something of his power, majesty and wisdom. Yet although nature is a signpost to God, it seems to be a rather vague one. Not everybody hears its voice and we learn nothing from nature of how to find God or of what he expects from us.

**A SECOND WAY** that God speaks is through his written Word. The Christian belief is that, over centuries, God sent messages through prophets about who he is, who we are and how to know him. Those messages are preserved for us in the Old and New Testaments of the Bible and they set out clearly who God is, who we are and how we can know him.

There are, however, limits to what the written word can communicate. If you've ever had a long correspondence with someone without meeting them you will realise how inadequate words on a page are. The Christian view is that God has also spoken in a third way and that is by coming in person through Jesus Christ. The Bible describes Jesus as 'the Word made flesh' and as God revealing himself in a way that we can all understand. This is spelt out in the very first verses of the New Testament letter to the Hebrews. 'In the past God spoke to our ancestors through the prophets at many times and in various ways, but in these last days he has spoken to us by his Son, whom he appointed heir of all things, and through whom also he made the universe. The Son is the radiance of God's glory and the exact representation of his being, sustaining all things by his powerful word' (Hebrews 1:1–3).

There are two marvellously important things about Jesus. The first is that in Jesus God speaks to us about who he is in the clearest possible way. In Jesus we see God made flesh (John 1:14). The second is that we can personally know Jesus as a friend by putting our trust in him. Through the power of the Holy Spirit we live in him and he can live in us. In the light of this, when it comes to the question of how we can know about God, it's hard not to respond, 'What more do you want?'

# HOW CAN GOD THE FATHER, JESUS AND THE HOLY SPIRIT BE ONE?

This question is all about what Christians call the Trinity and I'm not convinced that it *can* be explained in a way that we can fully understand it. However, let me do my best.

At the heart of the Trinity are three simple statements that Christians believe:

- There is only one God.

- The Father, Son, and Holy Spirit are each distinct persons.

- Each person is fully God.

Each of these statements contributes to the idea of the Trinity. The difficulty comes in how they relate to each other. To my mind one of the easiest ways of trying to understand the Trinity is by saying that God is one in *what* he is but three in *who* he is.

Ultimately the idea of the Trinity is biblical. Although the Bible doesn't use the word *Trinity* (the word 'tri-unity' might actually be better), it makes statements that require it.

- One central and unshakeable feature of the Jewish faith is that God is one (see, for example, Deuteronomy 6:4; Exodus 20:3; Isaiah 45:18). Jesus himself agreed with this (see Mark 12:29 where he says, 'Hear, O Israel: the Lord our God, the Lord is one').

- The Bible speaks of the Father as God (Luke 10:21; 1 Corinthians 8:6; Philippians 1:2).

- Jesus is referred to as God (John 1:1–14; 20:28; Romans 9:5; Hebrews 1:1–3, 5, 8; Titus 2:13). He also makes claims that only God could make.[2] Despite the fact that most of the early Christians came from a Jewish background, they called Jesus by God's title 'Lord' and regularly prayed to him as God.

- The Holy Spirit is treated as God in Acts 5:3–4 and elsewhere is given all the characteristics of God (Matthew 12:32; 1 Corinthians 2:10; Hebrews 10:29).

- Father, Son and Holy Spirit are treated as equal in Matthew 28:19; 2 Corinthians 13:14 and 1 Peter 1:2.

Incidentally, some people criticise the Trinity using the mathematical formula $1 + 1 + 1 = 3$ saying that, on this basis, there must be three Gods, not one. Actually, if you are going to use mathematics, then what you could say is that the formula for the Trinity is actually like this: $1 \times 1 \times 1 = 1$!

2 The claims made by Jesus, and about him, that imply he was God, are things that Chris Walley and I covered at length in our book *Jesus Christ – The Truth*.

Very early on in the history of Christianity, church leaders discussed at great length who God was and how Father, Son and Holy Spirit were related to each other. These leaders didn't see themselves as thinking up some theoretical idea of how God 'might work' but instead were trying to understand what God had said about himself. Their conclusion was that this concept of the Trinity was the only way of explaining all the information that they had from the Bible. Despite its difficulty, the idea that God is a Trinity has been firmly stated as a core belief for all the main Christian denominations for at least 1,700 years.

The protest that the idea of the Trinity cannot be true because we cannot understand it is actually very naïve. There are all sorts of things in science and mathematics that are not simple to understand. For instance, if you were to ask a physicist whether light is a wave or a particle you would get the answer: *both*. Mathematicians are very happy talking about multiple dimensions when all we can really understand is three dimensions. Things out there in the real world can get complicated and I don't see why God should be any different.

In fact, this argument that the Trinity 'is too complex to be true' is one that can be turned on its head. Everybody who has seriously thought about the idea of a God who creates the universe and keeps it going has concluded that he must be greater than we can comprehend or understand. Given how complex reality is I think if there were some sort of simple explanation of who God is I, for one, would be very suspicious about it.

It's interesting that the idea of the Trinity is actually very helpful in solving a number of problems. For example, if there is a God who is just one and who exists in glorious isolation then how, in the absence of 'God the Spirit' or 'God the Son', does he reveal himself to us? And given that to be 'a person' must mean that you communicate with someone, then if God exists on his own, who did he talk to before the world was created?

You may feel that I haven't satisfactorily answered the question of explaining how God the Father, Jesus and the Holy Spirit can be one. The reason, however, is simple: it's beyond our full understanding. But it doesn't worry me. As someone has said, 'If God was small enough for my brain to fully understand, he wouldn't be big enough to save me!'

# WHAT WAS GOD DOING BEFORE THE UNIVERSE BEGAN?

In most of the answers here I have tried to stay as close as possible to what I am fairly confident about. Here, however, I need to warn you that I have had to be a bit more speculative than I would like. The fact is that with a question like this we need to be very cautious about giving answers for at least two reasons.

**THE FIRST REASON** is that quite simply God hasn't revealed what he was doing before the universe began. I am reminded of Deuteronomy 29:29: 'The secret things belong to the LORD our God, but the things revealed belong to us and to our children for ever, that we may follow all the words of this law.' And it's a good rule that where God has chosen to be silent, we shouldn't, as it were, 'put words into his mouth'.

**THE SECOND REASON** is that here, as with many questions to do with God, we have to avoid slipping into what I call the 'Bearded-Old-Man-on-the-Clouds' nonsense. This is any sort of view that treats God as nothing more than some bigger human being and, on that basis, someone we can fairly easily understand. It is true that because God made us in 'his image', we can, to some extent, connect with him. There is a sense that he and we are 'on the same wavelength'. Nevertheless, we must always remember that an enormous gap between him and us still exists. God remains *God* – an eternal, all-powerful being who is infinitely beyond our understanding. The reality is that, even if God did reveal what he was doing before the creation, we might not be able to understand it. Centuries ago, Saint Augustine suggested that one of the things that God created when he made the universe was time itself. (No, I can't get my head around that either.) So, to talk about 'before' the creation of the universe may not actually make sense.

With those cautions noted, let me offer some thoughts.

One idea which can be rejected is that God got so bored by being alone that he decided to create the universe and human beings. The fact is, God doesn't need anything, not even the universe. Actually, the Christian view is that God wasn't ever alone. After all, he is Trinity: three persons – Father, Son and Holy Spirit – who are all united together. Although it's impossible for us to understand all that this means, one thing it *does* mean is that even before anything was created there would have been love and community between all three members of the Trinity. No one got bored. Equally, it's also worth remembering that there is not just God and his universe but a whole realm of angelic beings about whom we know very little: good and bad angels and those mysterious cherubim and seraphim. Did they exist before the creation of the world? Is that when Satan rebelled and evil began? I don't know but I'm not going to rule it out.

What we do have are hints of some things that occurred before the creation of the universe. Three Bible verses are relevant here.

- John 17:24: 'Father, I want those you have given me to be with me where I am, and to see my glory, the glory you have given me because you loved me before the creation of the world.'

- Ephesians 1:4: 'For he chose us in him before the creation of the world to be holy and blameless in his sight.'

- Titus 1:2: 'In the hope of eternal life, which God, who does not lie, promised before the beginning of time.'

Taking these verses together I think it's perfectly reasonable to suggest that, working together, the Trinity planned the creation and development of the universe. I rather like the idea that they spent time designing such things as hummingbirds, sketching out the shape of continents and planning how things were going to work out, even to the extent of the destinies of individuals like you and me.

Ultimately, though, we simply don't know what God was doing before the universe was created. My suggestion is that we are far better off thinking about how we can best live in the present and the future than worrying about a past that we cannot even begin to imagine.

# IS EVERYTHING POSSIBLE FOR GOD?

This sounds a simple question but in fact it raises deep issues that require us to do some thinking.

It's not hard to find claims in the Bible that God is omnipotent; that is, he can do all things. So, for instance, in Matthew 19:26 Jesus says, 'With God all things are possible.' There are many other verses which make similar claims, for example Luke 1:37 and 18:27, and there are numerous other verses which talk about God as being 'the Almighty'; in other words, someone who can do everything.

This idea of God being able to do everything has two separate aspects.

THE FIRST is that, because God is infinite, the extraordinary and almighty Being who made the universe in the past and keeps it going in the present, he has the *power* to do whatever he wants. If God wanted to add a new star to the sky he could do so without any problem.

THE SECOND aspect is that as the Lord, the maker and owner of the universe, God has the *authority* to do whatever he wants. In a legal sense, this entire universe belongs to him.

To borrow a neat phrase, we can say that God has both the *might* and the *right* to do what he wants. That is certainly seen in practice. The Bible describes how God has used his power over everything: the world, the weather, nations and individuals, whether emperors or peasants. The Bible goes even further in stating that God has power over everything, including every other supernatural being (for example, Romans 8:38–39). There are no gods, only the one God.

On the surface, then, it looks as though God can indeed 'do everything'. Yet on closer examination it's not quite that simple and it is obvious that there are things that God *can't* do and things that God *won't* do. The result is that we end up having to say something like: 'God can do everything that is possible for him to do given who he is.'

Let me explain why it is phrased like this. For one thing, God *can't* do what is nonsense or meaningless. Consider

some of the questions that philosophers have posed in the past about what God could do: 'Can he make a triangle with four sides?', 'Can he produce a rock too heavy for him to lift?' or 'Can he make 2+2 = 6?' The simple fact is that God can't do any of these things, not because he doesn't have the power or the authority but because they make no sense. No one, not even God, can make sense out of nonsense.

We can, however, go further and identify other things that God can't or won't do. In the 'can't' category are those actions that God can't do precisely because being God makes them impossible. So God can't create someone more powerful than himself, he can't fail in what he plans to do and he can't be taken by surprise. These are 'limitations' on God that are, in fact, incredibly encouraging. Equally helpful is the thought that because God is all-powerful, he cannot be manipulated, threatened or made to do anything that he does not want to do. God remains God!

Perhaps more importantly for us, there are things that God *won't* do because they are against his character. He is a holy God, committed to justice, full of love and faithful to his own promises. So for instance, we read in the Old Testament that 'God is not human, that he should lie, not a human being, that he should change his mind' (Numbers 23:19), a thought echoed in the New Testament (2 Timothy 2:11–13 and Titus 1:2). This idea that God is unchangeable and totally truthful is vital because it encourages us to trust God. After all, to follow Christ is not just to put our faith in him for a few years, but for all eternity. If we are going to trust God, we need to be reassured that he isn't going to suddenly change his mind.

The importance of the fact that God cannot, or will not change his mind or contradict himself is increased when we think of the idea of a *covenant*; something that is central to both the Old and the New Testaments. (In fact, a *testament* is another, older word for a covenant.) A covenant can be seen as being a legally binding treaty or agreement between two parties: in the Bible's case, between God and his people. In the covenants of the Bible, God solemnly promises to protect his people as long as they keep their side of the covenant, which is to obey him. Because God is utterly trustworthy, a covenant is of tremendous value. But if we felt that, at any point, God could change his mind and tear up his agreement or could be pressured to break it, then it would be worthless. An eternal covenant needs to be eternally unbreakable and it can only be that if God is all-powerful.

If we are to trust God with all we are, we need to have a God whom we can trust. The fact that God is all-powerful means that we can safely and confidently put our faith in him. He can be trusted both for this life and for eternity.

# DOES GOD KNOW THE FUTURE?

'Does God know the future?' is a question that, whether you have thought about it or not, is actually very important. Globally, we are increasingly aware of the vulnerability of the world and the uncertainty of the future. Is God taken by surprise by some virus? Does he know how much the climates are going to change? Is he aware of when the next tsunami is going to strike? Does he wonder who's going to win the next election? Does God lie awake at night, worrying about what may or may not happen on this little planet?

This matter about God's knowledge of the future has, of course, also a personal dimension because it applies to our own lives. We all face many kinds of uncertainties: health, wealth, careers, love and tragedy. I'm sure I'm not alone in thinking that when, say, our house is broken into or our child is injured or we get a bad medical test result, we all want a little bit more from God than an 'Oh dear! I'm awfully sorry. You know that took me by surprise too.' To put our faith in God – and certainly to pray to him for advice – is only really worth doing if he knows the future. If God is as much in the dark about the future as we are then there doesn't seem a lot of point in praying to him for our health or for wisdom in decision-making.

Whether God knows the future is particularly important in Christianity because it's a faith that is based on personal trust. In the Christian faith, God offers us a covenant – that solemn binding agreement I talked about whereby we agree to follow him and he promises to look after us forever. For example, Jesus promised this at the end of Matthew's gospel: 'And surely I am with you always, to the very end of the age.' In other words, God makes wonderful promises to look after his children but if he doesn't know the future then somewhere there ought to be a clause in the covenant along the lines of 'unforeseen events may render this agreement invalid'.

And that changes everything. After all, we have all heard of people who, having been promised some brilliant investment policy or an awesome holiday, find that it never materialises due to 'unanticipated circumstances'. One of the big themes of the Bible is that God is someone you can trust with everything and everybody you hold dear. Speaking personally, if God doesn't know the future, I'm not sure that I can trust him that far.

Thankfully, the Bible clearly states that God knows the future. I think of such verses as Isaiah 46:10: 'I make known the end from the beginning, from ancient times, what is still to come. I say, "My purpose will stand, and I will do all that I please."' Equally, in Psalm 139:4 we read, 'Before a word is on my tongue you, LORD, know it completely', and in verse 16, 'Your eyes saw my unformed body; all the days ordained for me were written in your book before one of them came to be.' Another verse is Jeremiah 29:11: '"For I know the plans I have for you," declares the LORD, "plans to prosper you and not to harm you, plans to give you hope and a future."' The New Testament echoes these ideas (see, for example, John 16:13; Ephesians 1:11; 2:10; 1 John 3:20).

So I'm convinced that God knows the future. However, that does raise other questions.

ONE IS, how can God know the future if it hasn't happened yet? The standard answer here is that God is 'outside time', something that we've already touched on. It's not an easy concept but perhaps it helps if we think of the relationship between an author and the book he or she has written. They know what is going to happen and can see it all from beginning to end in front of them. Similarly with God: from his perspective he can see the past, the present and the future.

**A SECOND QUESTION** – and it's a big one – is whether the fact that God knows the future means that there is no choice and everything is somehow predestined so that we have no real freedom about what we do. Here again the Bible is clear that we do have choice (see, for example, Joshua 24:15; John 7:17; Galatians 5:13; Revelation 3:20) and that we are not programmed robots, but instead responsible beings. Although it's not easy to get our head around that idea, I think it's perfectly possible that God can know the future and that we can have the ability to choose how we act. To see what our choices will be before we make them is not the same as making those choices for us.

I'm very glad that the one I worship knows the future. I'm not sure I want a God who takes risks with my world. Or with me.

# HOW CAN GOD LISTEN TO EVERYBODY'S PRAYERS ALL AT ONCE?

Even the best of us struggle to handle more than one conversation at a time. 'Hang on!' we say when someone phones us when we are in a meeting, 'let me get back to you – I'm talking to someone else.' This raises an obvious problem: how does God handle everybody's prayers at once?

One easy answer would be that he doesn't; that there are times where quite simply there's just too much going on even for God. I think that's completely wrong because the Bible tells us that not only does God treat prayer very seriously, he cares for us as individuals (see Psalm 139:1–4; Ezra 8:21–23; Nehemiah 2:1–5; Matthew 6:5–8). The Bible confidently declares that we can know God as our heavenly parent and that carries with it the idea that he cares for us as the ideal father or mother does for every one of their children. So God must have a way of answering prayer or he would be failing with his parenting.

But how does he do it? Let's imagine what you might call a 'worst-case scenario'. There's a big earthquake and even before the rumbling and shaking has died away, there are thousands, perhaps tens of thousands, of urgent prayers going up to God, all at the same time. How on earth – or in heaven – does he manage it? Some people seem to imagine that God has something rather like a glorified answerphone system and, when he has a moment, checks up on the backlog of calls. I don't find that either believable or encouraging. If I'm in a plane and the engines fail, I'd prefer God to respond before we hit the ground. And in any circumstance, I really don't want to receive an answer to a prayer along the lines of 'I'm afraid I'm busy at the moment and all my lines are engaged. Remember, your call is valuable to me and I'll get back to you as soon as possible.'

In trying to answer this problem I want to say that we avoid what I called earlier the 'Bearded-Old-Man-on-the-Clouds' nonsense. As the Bible repeatedly teaches, God is not simply a human being with extraordinary powers, but a being who is infinitely greater than we can imagine or understand (see Psalm 147:5; Job 26:14; Isaiah 40:28; 55:8–9). In fact the answer here, as with a number of other questions, surely lies with the idea that God is 'outside time' so that what you and I feel and measure as minutes, hours and days does not pass for him in the same unstoppable and continuous way that it does for us.

This is not an easy concept but let me suggest one way of thinking about this. When we watch a film, what we are seeing is lots of individual frames that appear on the screen one after the other (normally at 24 frames per second) to give the impression of a fluid stream of action. In theory someone could stop that stream of images, isolate a single individual frame within it and then look at it for as long as they wanted. From God's point of view, 'our' reality may be like this only a billion or trillion times more complex. Nevertheless, it means that he would be able to hear every prayer and give it the attention it deserves.

I find this idea tremendously encouraging because it says that when we come to prayer, God will give us as much time as we need. When we are praying it's all too easy to think of God as being some enormously pressured Supreme Managing Director of Everything who is so busy trying to handle a billion tasks at once that all we can hope for is the briefest moment of his time. It just doesn't work like that. God takes our praying seriously: let's do the same!

# WAS JESUS GOD?

To ask whether Jesus is God is perhaps the most important of all the questions posed in this book. If Jesus was indeed more than a man and, in some way, God, then he becomes supremely important. He is alive, he knows who we are, what we are doing, what we are thinking and what our future is. As God he has authority to forgive, to heal and to rescue. He is someone who can be trusted completely in every situation, whatever life (and death) brings us.

Precisely because the idea that Jesus is God is of such overwhelming importance it has often been challenged. To be honest, many people are happier with a Jesus who is a long-dead prophet than a Jesus who is alive and all-powerful. Yet for nearly 2,000 years, mainstream Christianity has – against innumerable attacks – held firmly to the belief that Jesus is someone whom we can know as God.

One common means of trying to undermine the deity of Jesus is to assume that over the years his reputation grew because of some kind of 'wishful thinking'. So, the theory goes, Jesus was originally no more than some sort of prophet but, with the passage of time, his followers 'promoted' him from being 'a man who was good' to 'the man who was God'. History, however, will not allow us this option. For instance, we find extraordinary statements about Jesus in the letters of the New Testament where language that Jews would have used only for God is applied, without hesitation or qualification, to Jesus. He is 'Lord', he rules over everything, he is in heaven, he can be worshipped and prayed to. Some of these letters can be confidently dated within twenty years of the events of the first Easter. Outside the New Testament, we have a letter written in AD 112 by Pliny the Elder, a governor in what is now Turkey, to the Roman Emperor Trajan which mentions that Christians were 'worshipping Christ as God'.

The divinity of Jesus was not accepted without careful thought. For several hundred years church leaders carefully thought about what this claim meant and how, if Jesus was considered to be God, God could still be one. The answer they came up with is the Trinity: something that I have discussed in the question 'How can God the Father, Jesus and the Holy Spirit be one?' (page 44).

So why did so many devout Jewish people, upholders of a faith in which linking anything with God was blasphemy, consider that Jesus could be treated as God? The answer is found in the gospels, where we read about what Jesus of Nazareth said and did. In the book *Jesus Christ – The Truth* that Chris Walley and I wrote, we discuss not only the strong evidence for the authenticity of the gospels but also the identity of Jesus. Let me summarise here just some of the evidence for Jesus being God.

- Jesus accepted titles that were only used of God. He frequently referred to himself as the 'Son of God', as 'the Son of Man' (a term with implications of being divine) and as the eternal 'I am'. The angry reaction that his use of some of these terms produced indicates they were considered blasphemous.

- Jesus made claims and acted in a way that implied he was, in some way, God. So, for example, he declared that he personally was making a new covenant between God and the human race. He claimed to forgive people, to have existed in the past, to have authority over the temple, the Kingdom and God's Law. Perhaps most remarkably, Jesus stated that, at the end of time, he personally would judge the world.

- Jesus claimed unity with God, saying, 'Anyone who has seen me has seen the Father' (John 14:9–10).

- Jesus performed miraculous actions that only God could do. He stilled storms, walked on water, exorcised demons, accomplished extraordinary healings and multiplied food. Particularly striking is the fact that nowhere in performing these deeds is there any reference to Jesus praying to God to ask him to do them. With an extraordinary personal authority, Jesus just did them himself.

- Whenever the Old Testament talks of prophets and what they preached we read the lines of 'the Word of the Lord came to X' or how prophet Y began his message with such words as 'God says'. The message of the prophets is always, as it were, 'second-hand'. Yet we never read anything like this of Jesus: he just says 'I say' or 'truly I tell you'. Indeed, at the start of John's gospel we are told that Jesus personally is the Word of God.

It is true that in the gospels Jesus only rarely makes an open claim to be God. This is in fact part of a pattern in which Jesus at first avoids directly stating that he is God but instead increasingly does and says things which, to those who are thinking about what is happening, present unmistakable but indirect claims to be God. Finally, at his trial Jesus is open in his claims to be God. Indeed, after the resurrection Jesus openly accepts worship (John 20:28).

There is one other argument about the divinity of Jesus that is often overlooked. Almost no historian, whether Christian or not, doubts that Jesus was crucified, apparently at the request of the religious leaders. Why did he arouse such hostility? We read of no comparable hatred against John the Baptist, who preached against the religious authorities in the strongest possible terms. The reason that Jesus was crucified was because the leaders believed that he had committed blasphemy for which death was the required punishment.

Finally, can I point out that whether or not Jesus was God is the ultimate in decisive questions. If Jesus claimed to be God but wasn't, then he was either deranged or a deceiver and so *nothing* he said can be trusted. If, on the other hand, as Christians have always believed, Jesus not only claimed to be God but *was* God then every human quest for ultimate meaning ends with him. Jesus is all we need to know God. But if we do come to the verdict that Jesus is indeed God, the question now shifts from him to us. What are we going to do about Jesus?

# PART THREE

# QUESTIONS ABOUT GOD, GOOD AND EVIL

Many of the questions we are thinking about here are interesting and intriguing. So, for example, I suspect only a very few people lie awake at night fretting about what they will be wearing in heaven. Yet not all questions are so lightly treated. For instance, I know that many people agonise deeply and frequently over how a good God can allow suffering and injustice.

In this section I want to look at some of these questions. But before I do, let me give you a warning. The first is that the problem of why evil occurs if a good, wise and all-powerful God does exist, is by every estimate one of the strongest arguments against the Christian faith. To make any response here is challenging, not only because it is a hard and complicated subject but because it touches on deep and personal pains. We all know cases where suffering, in the form of a stroke, a car accident or a cancer has suddenly occurred, bringing unexpected agony to what seem to be blameless lives. Pain and suffering are not simply academic matters to be discussed in the cool language of logic or philosophy: they involve situations where people scream in mental or physical pain. Anyone who chooses to talk or write about these things needs to tread very sensitively indeed.

Nevertheless, precisely because these questions are so important, we need to explore them.

# WHY DOES GOD ALLOW EVIL?

The problem of evil and suffering is *the* big argument against Christianity. Whether suffering involves sick babies, grieving mothers or crippling injuries, it raises the most serious of questions. Why does a good and all-powerful God allow evil? Why doesn't he just simply end that disease, heal that suffering child, stop that motorbike accident? Let me be as honest and specific as possible: why did God allow millions of people to die in the Nazi concentration camps when the simple act of giving Hitler a much-merited heart attack could have ended it all?

Right at the start it's vital to recognise that this is a problem that people only really seriously raise with Christians. The reason for this is that we claim not only that there is an all-powerful God but that he is a loving God. In fact, a better version of the question we are examining would be why does a *wise and loving* God allow evil? You could understand the existence of evil if God wasn't entirely in control of the universe or if there were several different gods battling it out amongst themselves. Equally, evil would be unsurprising if there was a God who was cruel or merely apathetic about the world. It's only if, as Christians claim, you have a God who is all-wise, all-powerful and loving that we have this question. In fact, to turn the question on its head it's important to note that, if you are an atheist, strictly speaking there isn't a problem of evil at all. Why not? Quite simply because 'evil' doesn't exist: it's just the way the world works. Don't take my word for it. Take that of atheist Richard Dawkins who has written that in the universe there is 'no design, no purpose, no evil, no good, nothing but pitiless indifference'. This raises the question for the atheist as to why everybody recognises evil exists and is shocked by it, when according to atheism evil doesn't exist.

Nevertheless, let's go back to Christianity and evil. But before I give you some reasons why evil might occur, let me point out the fact that this is not a new question. In fact, over the last 2,000 years almost every generation of Christians has endured more suffering and evil than we have. Take the great eighteenth-century composer and devout Christian J.S. Bach. He had twenty children, of whom only ten survived into adulthood; on returning home from a trip he found that his much-loved wife had died and had been buried in his absence.

Now that's suffering. In considering a world in which wars, premature deaths, plagues, starvation and violence occur, Christians have come up with different responses to the problem of why these things occur. Let me summarise five of them.

**REASON 1:** Evil is a result of the world's rebellion against God

The Bible is very clear that this world is not how God intended it to be. It is a rebellious planet and from the start human beings have chosen to disobey God's commands. The result of this is a twisted or 'fallen' creation that we must live with. Disobedience has a price and much – but not all – evil is due to human rebelliousness or, to use a shorter word, *sin*. Whether you agree with that or not it is undeniable that if the world was a fairer, wiser and kinder place, many of the effects of natural disasters and diseases would be reduced. Flooding becomes worse because greed has allowed building in vulnerable places; earthquakes kill more people because poverty has resulted in poorly built houses; diseases spread further because vaccination programmes have been rejected or are unaffordable.

**REASON 2:** God can use evil to demonstrate goodness

Someone might praise the love that a young, healthy couple show for each other on the day of their marriage. Great! But let's fast forward forty years when wrinkles, arthritis, baldness, fat and a host of ailments have taken hold. Yet they still love each other: so isn't this battered but enduring love now even more praiseworthy? It's hard to imagine the meaning of words such as *courage, loyalty* and *sacrifice* except where there has been some sort of struggle against evil. Light shines brightest in darkness, kindness stands out best in the face of cruelty and truth is most praiseworthy in a time of lies.

**REASON 3**: God can use bad things for our good

The Bible tells us that God is not content with his children as we are. He is constantly at work to change those who take the name of Christ in order to make them more and more like him. Unfortunately, we are all disinclined to change and sometimes gentle persuasion is not enough. When you are trying to free some fixed object in the house it's not uncommon to give up using a small tool and, as a last resort, reach instead for the hammer and apply brute force. That principle applies to our lives. Sometimes, in order to produce change God needs to resort to allowing pain and suffering.

Experience tells us that it's easy to remain arrogant and to reject God until something really unpleasant happens to us: only then do we treat him seriously. Hebrews 12 in the Bible talks about how God uses hardship as a tool of discipline to make his people what he wants them to be. Children cling more closely to their parents in the dark; God's children cling closer to him when they are suffering.

Joni Eareckson Tada lived a very active life all through her growing-up years. She enjoyed riding horses, hiking, tennis and swimming. On July 30th, 1967, she dived into Chesapeake Bay after misjudging the shallowness of the water. She suffered a fracture between the fourth and fifth cervical vertebrae in her neck and became a quadriplegic (or tetraplegic), paralysed from the shoulders down.

Joni, a Christian, wrote: 'Sometimes God permits what he hates and uses it to accomplish what he loves.'

Joni is the author of forty-eight books on the subjects of disability and Christianity.

**REASON 4**: Evil reminds us that this world is not our home

Imagine that you were living a prosperous life, free from all aches and pains in some comfortable part of the world. It would be lovely, but you might be tempted to think that you were already in paradise and that is a very dangerous state of mind. Life for the Christian is like travelling on a long plane journey where you break your journey on route or change planes at another airport. However tired you are, you have to remind yourself at this point that you're not there yet: this is merely a temporary stopover. So it is with life. Evil and pain remind us (and we need reminding) that we have not yet arrived at our destination and that we need to keep pressing on until Jesus himself tells us that it's all over. We are not home yet.

**REASON 5**: We only see a tiny part of the story

'Why does God allow evil?' is actually an inadequate question and what we really ought to do is rewrite it to ask, 'Why does God allow evil *in this life?*' From a Christian point of view, we need to think in terms of eternity: of time stretching on without end. To do that is to realise that what happens here in this life is utterly trivial compared to the years of eternity. Even if we were to have a life full of pain, it would still count as insignificant against knowing and enjoying God in paradise forever.

So those are five reasons but I don't want to stop there. A key thing about the problem of evil is that explaining it in terms of theology or philosophy is not the best approach. To deal with suffering is not to engage in a philosophical form of Sudoku in which we scratch our brains trying to come up with an adequate response. It is to encounter a painful reality that demands a practical response. It is here perhaps in the darkness of suffering we see the glory of Christianity. In the face of human suffering God did not merely offer us encouraging and comforting words; he looked on our misery and sent his Son Jesus to rescue us by himself enduring suffering. In imitation, we should look on the misery of others and seek to do what we can either to prevent evil from happening or, if it's happened, to try to heal it.

Let me end with a fascinating and challenging example of responding to the problem of evil. Dr Denis Mukwege is a gynaecologist in the Democratic Republic of the Congo and also a church leader. Dr Mukwege specialises in the repair and healing of women who have been wounded in specific and brutally horrid ways in the course of conflict. His work has been so significant that, in 2018, he was awarded the Nobel Peace Prize. Ultimately, this is the best response to evil: don't be preoccupied with its origins – do something about it!

# WHY ARE THERE EARTHQUAKES, VOLCANOES AND TSUNAMIS?

This is something of a follow-on from the previous question about why God allows evil but it is such a major topic that I think it's worth looking at on its own.

A somewhat frequent habit of people is to talk on subjects about which they know little! So here I consulted a geologist friend. He pointed out that Earth is remarkably suitable for life. That ability to host abundant life is something that we shouldn't take for granted. It doesn't take much for a planet to become a barren desert: consider for example either Mars which is airless and freezing cold or Venus which has a surface temperature hot enough to melt lead.

For a planet to be stable and suitable for life is far from easy. In fact our Earth is like a spaceship in which various processes continuously operate so that everything is recycled, with the result that vital chemicals in the atmosphere, the oceans and on the land are not removed for ever but go back into circulation. So although nutrients and chemicals descend to the bottom of the sea and are apparently lost to the world of life, Earth is an active planet and as oceans close and mountains rise, those vital chemicals are brought up back into circulation through volcanoes and erosion. Our world is constantly refreshing and renewing itself.

This is wonderful but the principle of 'no pain, no gain' applies here: there is a price to pay for having an active planet and that price involves earthquakes, volcanoes and tsunamis and, less spectacularly, wind and rain. It's a global example of the principle that everything of value has the potential to be a hazard: fire can burn us, sunlight can harm us and even food can choke us. Nevertheless, I think we'd all prefer a living planet with risks, to a dead planet without them.

However, it's not simply a case of blaming the natural state of things. The world is not what it was supposed to be: evil exists and human beings – and the world itself – are disconnected from God.

What we can say with confidence is that we human beings haven't helped matters. We can now predict with some accuracy *where* earthquakes, volcanoes, tsunamis and landslides are likely to occur and even to some extent *when* they will occur. So we aren't exactly helpless but we aren't doing as much as we could do. For instance, the most obvious thing to do would be to find the areas that are at high risk from these problems and, instead of building on or near them, simply leave them to nature. And if we must build, we should build wisely and sensibly. Today's engineering means that the tallest skyscrapers can be built so that even a big earthquake will do little more than shake them. It's also worth noting that often it's not the actual natural disaster, whether it be an earthquake or tsunami, that kills people but the disease and malnutrition that occur after it. And dealing with victims of natural disasters is something that we can do something about. But to do that costs money and many of the poor countries who face risks in these areas simply cannot afford that. I have no doubt that if the world didn't spend so much money on trying to make bigger and better bombs, if there wasn't so much corruption and if we all shared our wealth around a bit more, then we could reduce casualties caused by natural disasters to a fraction of what they are today.

This allows me to end on an important point. As I suggested at the end of the response to the previous question, the theoretical discussion of human suffering is not the most important matter: doing something about it is. The phrase 'don't just stand there and do nothing' doesn't just apply to specific incidents; it should be a principle that rules our lives.

# WHY DO SOME GOOD PEOPLE DIE YOUNG AND SOME BAD PEOPLE LIVE A LONG TIME?

This is another question linked to the problem of evil and it focuses on the sad but universally recognised fact that this world seems completely unfair. Let's focus our thinking with two imaginary but typical examples. Somewhere, a promising doctor in her twenties, walking home to her family at the end of a long day saving lives, is crushed to death by a drunk driver. At the same moment, a seventy-year-old millionaire who has made his fortune through fraud and bullying, pops open the champagne on his yacht with his latest mistress. The problem is obvious. If there is a God who is in charge of the universe and who cares deeply about right and wrong, what's he up to?

As I mentioned earlier, it's important to realise that these issues of suffering and injustice aren't just theoretical questions that we can calmly discuss over a coffee. For those involved they overflow with tearstained grief and angry bitterness. And, of course, they don't have to be as dramatic as the examples I've just given. We all know of people whose career failed because someone else took the credit, of wives or husbands who were cheated and left – possibly quite literally – holding the baby, and of entrepreneurs who made fortunes by defrauding the public. So here I want to say that if some injustice or tragedy has happened to you, then let me offer you my sympathies. These are not trivial matters.

Before going any further I think it's important to point out once more the striking fact that these issues of 'divine injustice' are only really an argument against the God of Christianity, a being who is not only all-powerful but also loving and committed to the triumph of right over wrong. Only here is injustice a problem. After all, if the universe is controlled only by random chance, then what you and I feel as being a monumental unfairness is merely 'just the way the dice rolled' and ought to be treated with a shrug of the shoulders. Similarly, if everything is the product of some 'Cosmic Architect' who, having set the universe in motion, walked away and left it to its own devices, there isn't an issue either. Equally, if God is some cold, compassionless tyrant, all you can say is, 'What happens, happens. *Tough!*'

Actually, the fact that even non-Christians feel a sense of outrage at injustice is very striking. It is as if, deep down, we all acknowledge the existence of a good and caring God and realise that there is something very wrong about the brutal and unjust character of reality.

This is another tough question but let me give you some thoughts on what we might call 'the problem of injustice' that may help.

- While we might want to blame God for being unfair, the Bible tells us that this is too simple. The picture it gives is of a God who is neither an uncaring engineer nor a cruel tyrant but rather someone who, like a loving parent, grieves over his broken creation. We are told that this world was created good and it is not how God meant it to be. The human race's action of defiance against God has given rise to consequences and some of what we suffer is simply because of this. This is a world whose wounds are largely self-inflicted. One day, we are promised, it will be remade, but not yet.

- We need to remember that we live in a story which is not yet completed. Although we tend to think of this life as being everything, Christianity tells us that, in reality, this world is merely a brief preliminary before eternity. Even the longest earthly life is nothing more than the first page of the unending volumes of eternal existence. One day, in a way that we cannot now understand, all that can be made right will be made right. We may be sure, too, that part of that process of restoration will be justice: as the old saying goes, there will be 'payday someday'. But our story is not finished: those who have followed Jesus can be assured that one day they will arrive at that place where there is both healing for pain and justice for injustice. Just read the end of the book of Revelation.

- We often misunderstand the purpose of life. Many people think that the only thing that matters in life is 'winning'. Actually, 'winning' in life – whatever that means – is, in the context of eternity, utterly trivial. The reality is that God is not interested in whether we win or lose in the game of life but only how we 'play the game'.

- If you accept that the most important thing in life is having and enjoying a living relationship with God then it's an odd fact that crises and difficulties are more effective at bringing us close to him than prosperity. Christian teaching has always said that God uses pain and suffering to shape his children into what he wants them to be (Hebrews 12:7). In my experience some of the most impressive Christians I know are not those who have prospered in life, but those who have suffered. As always, a light shines more clearly when it is placed in darkness.

Finally, it's worth mentioning that if we have put our faith in Christ then God himself goes with us through every injustice and every suffering. Indeed, the cross of Jesus tells us that God himself knows an awful lot about suffering.

# WHY CAN PEOPLE DO BAD THINGS AND GOD DOESN'T SEEM TO PUNISH THEM?

'Why do good things happen to bad people?' is the other side of the coin of the more common question, 'Why do bad things happen to good people?' It's a fair question. Why, if there is a just and loving God, do evil people often seem to get off scot free? Let's take the character currently at Number One in the 'Bad People List', the thoroughly nasty Joseph Stalin who led Russia for thirty years and who was certainly responsible for at least ten million deaths and probably twice or three times that. Rather disappointingly for those who believe in any kind of justice in this life, he died quietly in his bed at the age of seventy-four.

There are an almost infinite number of similar cases where life doesn't seem fair. Not only is it quite common for bad people to escape any kind of obvious judgement but they often appear to do very nicely out of it all. For example, a good number of drug dealers prosper financially and enjoy long, untroubled retirements in glorious sun-drenched villas; many manipulative bullies successfully climb to the top of their professions on the bruised backs of those who work for them; and many operators of crooked businesses, having quietly defrauded thousands of people, end up in their comfortable twilight years being honoured as 'pillars of society'.

We are not helped here because popular fiction and Hollywood tend to feed us stories in which justice is done. You know the sort of thing: the abused heroine turns the tables on the villain so that he meets a suitably juicy end; the corrupt politician is publicly humiliated and sent to jail. We love such stories but sadly, reality often fails to match it. Justice is not always done. In fact, it's an interesting question to ask why, if the world is so obviously unjust, does everybody feel that there ought to be justice? The Christian answer would be because we all have a sense of right and wrong implanted in us by God. If you don't believe in God, I'm not sure that there *is* an answer.

In the face of this problem of injustice let me offer some comments.

FIRST, one important thing to say here is that throwing around words like 'good' and 'bad' with respect to people is not helpful. The Bible is clear that all of us are deeply flawed individuals; we have all chosen to run things our own way and have all rebelled against God. By God's standards there are no 'good' people. On that basis you could argue that the truly remarkable thing is that *any* of us enjoys any good thing in this life.

**SECOND**, we need to be a bit cautious in judging others. Who knows what you and I might have been like had we experienced trouble in our upbringing or made some unwise choice of friends? Equally, sometimes the only thing that prevents people from committing great sin is a lack of opportunity. I suspect most of us are not guilty of slavery, arms dealing or corruptly governing entire countries. But, if we'd had the opportunity, would we have been?

**THIRD**, the idea that *most* bad people enjoy long, happy and prosperous lives may be a myth. The Old Testament is clear: to obey the Lord brings blessings. These are normally wealth, peace, family and length of years (Leviticus 26:3–13; Deuteronomy 28:1–14) and, in contrast, to disobey God and break his laws – to be 'wicked' – is to face judgement in various ways (Leviticus 26:14–39; Deuteronomy 28:15–68). Mind you, even in the Old Testament, this ruling is not entirely a hundred per cent. Even there some good people die young and some bad people live on into old age. In the New Testament, however, there is a shift in focus from physical benefits in this world, to spiritual benefits in this world and physical ones in the next. Nevertheless, on balance, the Old Testament principle holds true: wickedness invites judgement in this life. There *is* a rough justice in this life: cheats, bullies and liars generally do not prosper over the long term. Actually, where they do seem to have achieved success, it is often poisoned for them and they do not enjoy what they have sought. So, for example, many people find that ill-gotten wealth brings with it a troubled conscience and ill-gained power is accompanied by enemies and unease. Many of those who are very wealthy describe feelings of emptiness and discontent: they have climbed life's summit only to find that there is nothing there. In my experience, there is often more joy in an impoverished African village than in any gathering of the super-rich. It's worth also remembering that wealth grants you no immunity to health and death; indeed, having more things often brings fewer years.

FOURTH – and it's a sadly overlooked point – when God gives us good things, he watches what we do with them. A blessing is always a testing. This principle is actually taught by Jesus in the striking (and uncomfortable) parable of the rich man and Lazarus (Luke 16:19–31). It's an account of a rich man who does nothing for the beggar Lazarus at his gates and when both men die, the rich man finds himself in hell and the beggar in heaven. The rich man appeals to Abraham, as the father of the Jewish people, only to get the chilling response, 'Son, remember that in your lifetime you received your good things, while Lazarus received bad things, but now he is comforted here and you are in agony.' There is another thought-provoking challenge about the risks of riches in Luke 12:48, 'From everyone who has been given much, much will be demanded; and from the one who has been entrusted with much, much more will be asked.' To rework the well-known quote, we could say that 'with great riches comes great responsibility'. I believe that on the Day of Judgement God will ask those of us who have been given a lot, 'And what did you do with what I gave you?'

FINALLY, we must consider the point that I have made in previous answers: *we only see a tiny part of the real story*. Our question, 'Why can people do bad things and God doesn't seem to punish them?' should have three little words added at the end: '*in this life*'. We need to have an eternal perspective and remember that even the longest life on this earth is a blink of an eye in terms of the endlessness that is eternity. Interestingly, the question of the prosperous wicked is raised at length in Psalm 73 where the writer complains, 'For I envied the arrogant when I saw the prosperity of the wicked. They have no struggles; their bodies are healthy and strong. They are free from common human burdens; they are not plagued by human ills' (verses 3–5). He wrestles with this and the way that it makes him feel both envious and angry before he comes to the following answer: 'When I tried to understand all this, it troubled me deeply till I entered the sanctuary of God; then I understood their final destiny' (verses 16–17). That ominous little phrase 'their final destiny' should give us all pause for thought.

When we are faced with injustice of either undeserving prosperity or unmerited suffering, we must always remember that we have yet to see the big picture. And it's no bad thing to remind ourselves that from the point of view of most of the inhabitants of this planet we are the prosperous and wealthy. What are *we* going to do with what we have been given?

# PART FOUR

# BEING MADE RIGHT WITH GOD

One unhelpful and dangerous view of Christianity is to treat it as little more than a fascinating discussion topic to engage our thinking. Indeed, the way that questions are raised and then answered here might encourage someone to think of the Christian faith as little more than a philosophy that offers stimulating and challenging answers to some of life's deepest questions. Yet to do this is to misunderstand entirely what the Christian faith is all about. In reality, Christianity is not a series of theoretical ideas but something that is utterly practical: it is a medicine for the sick, a lifebelt for the drowning, a map for the lost and many more other vital and practical things.

The first preachers about Jesus borrowed an interesting word from their culture, *evangelion*, to refer to their message; a word that over time has given rise to our *evangelical* and *evangelist*. The word literally means 'good news' but before it was taken over by Christians it was used to describe an important and urgent official announcement, often sent out by the emperor himself. An *evangelion* was news announced with trumpets and shouts and it demanded our full attention. That importance and urgency is there in the Christian message. There is bad news: you and I are guilty before God and deserve punishment for our sins but, in the very same breath, there is the best of good news: God in Christ has substituted for us, taken our punishment for us and offers forgiveness and hope.

Christianity is about the most important topic of all: how can we come to know God? That's an extraordinary question that breeds more questions.

# HOW CAN THE DEATH OF A JEWISH PEASANT 2,000 YEARS AGO DO ANYTHING FOR ME TODAY?

Dealing with these questions make me feel as if I'm a batsman facing a rather inconsistent bowler. Some of the questions are so tough that all you can do is play them defensively but then every so often you get a ball bowled to you that demands to be hit for six. This is one of those.

Let me start by willingly admitting that if Jesus was an ordinary human being then his death would certainly not do anything for you or me. Yet the Bible proclaims that whatever adjectives we may use of Jesus, *ordinary* is not one of them. The Bible makes two vital and unique claims about Jesus and we need to think about both.

First, the Bible declares that, unlike anybody else who has ever lived, Jesus was without sin and therefore totally innocent and undeserving of death, that grim penalty for breaking God's law. Now if we make the obvious assumption that heaven operates on the basis of justice then this establishes the possibility that Jesus could, *in principle*, take the punishment for someone else. He could act as a substitute and so, to use technical theological language, *atonement* is possible. There is, however, a problem here that many people are willing to point out. Yes, an innocent man could take the punishment for another but only *one* other person. Surely justice demands that any exchange – any atonement – must be on a strict one-to-one basis. One innocent individual could save another human being but no more than that.

There is logic to this but it's here we need to note the second vital claim of the Bible: that Jesus was not just a man but, in a way beyond our full comprehension, also God. And as God, who has no limits, he could stand in for a limitless number of people. It is as if, in the great equation to do with the atonement, when we put Jesus into it, we are inserting an infinity symbol into the formula. (This, incidentally, is why Christians have defended the deity of Christ: if he was merely a good *man* then the idea of atonement would not work.) The fact that Jesus was both God and an innocent man means that his death has the most important significance possible.

Here, though, yet another objection could be raised. On what basis can Jesus stand in for you and for me? Isn't it rather immoral that an innocent man takes the punishment for other people? In fact, this is a problem that is probably only felt by those of us who live in the modern western world where we see ourselves as individuals, with each one of us standing or falling on our own. The fact is that in many parts of the world people identify themselves primarily in terms of belonging to a family and, in that context, one member of a family can stand in for another.

Given this, it is extremely significant that the Bible says that to put your faith in Jesus is to be adopted into his family (see Romans 8:15; 9:26; Galatians 3:26; Ephesians 1:5). In fact, when talking of being a believer, it refers to Jesus as our brother, as in Hebrews 2:11: 'Both the one who makes people holy and those who are made holy are of the same family. So Jesus is not ashamed to call them brothers and sisters.' As our elder brother, Jesus can stand in for those who have been adopted into his family and there is a perfect justice in him bearing the punishment of another brother or sister. It's family business.

So that's why the death of Jesus is important: it is the ultimate, perfect and final sacrifice that pays off the moral debts of all who have committed themselves to him. Yet the question threw in a little phrase 'a Jewish peasant 2,000 years ago' and I don't want to ignore it. One obvious point to make is that if God *was* to intervene personally in human history it would have to have been somewhere, at some time, with somebody. Yet there are other things I want to note and let me point out three of them.

FIRST, we are reminded that Jesus was Jewish. This is important. He was not, as it were, parachuted in from heaven like some total outsider, but came as the fulfilment of the long history of the Jewish people whom God had chosen and taught about himself. We frequently hear today the phrase 'backstory' to refer to the background or history to some individual or great event. The Old Testament is the long but essential backstory to Jesus and the cross. And as a Jew, Jesus was also born somewhere that could be considered to be as close to the centre of the world as anywhere: a point where the three great continents of Asia, Europe and Africa meet.

SECOND, the 'peasant' bit is important too. Given that throughout history most people, most of the time, have been 'peasants' of some sort, this makes Jesus and his teaching something that much of the world can easily relate to. It also emphasises his humility. That is a vital element in the Christian story, which is all about someone who, as God, was rich but who, for our sake, became poor (2 Corinthians 8:9; Philippians 2:6–11). It is a pointer, too, to the fact that to become a follower of Jesus requires humility; we must all bow before the one who is on the cross.

FINALLY, the '2,000 years ago' is also relevant. It reminds us that Jesus existed in the real history of our world. The Bible story is not set 'a long time ago in a galaxy far, far away . . .' or Middle Earth but in a very real place at a very real time.

In the cross everything comes together: our human sin which condemns us encounters the perfect balance of God's love and God's justice that saves us. 'How can the death of a Jewish peasant 2,000 years ago do anything for me today?' demands a challenging response: 'Who – or what else – is there that can save me?' No one else in the history of the world fits this requirement: only in Jesus do we find any hope of being saved.

# IF JESUS HAS PAID THE PRICE FOR MY SIN, WHY DO I NEED TO BE A GOOD PERSON?

On coming across something similar to what I have just written, many people come up with an obvious question: 'If Jesus died for me and by doing so paid for my sins, why do I need to bother to try to be good?' Understandably, the idea that someone could claim to be a child of God but continue to do all sorts of bad things has struck many people as outrageous. It also flies in the face of the New Testament which talks a lot about good behaviour on almost every page. Not only is this a good question but it's actually an important one: the link between 'being saved' and 'doing good things' has been a source of division within Christianity for centuries. I'm not sure I can bridge that division but let me try to set out some principles.

FIRST, we have to accept that doing good things cannot save us. Perfection is the entry requirement for heaven and as no one is perfect we are in trouble if we think and try to save ourselves. In fact, one of the problems with trying to be a good person is that, sooner or later, pride creeps in and in doing so completely undoes any progress towards perfection.

Equally, the idea that our good actions – 'our works' – can save us undermines what Jesus did on the cross. At its heart the message of the New Testament is God saying 'come and accept the wonderful free gift I have offered you'. All we need to do to be saved is: a) accept that Christ stood in our place and at the cross bore our judgement, b) confess and turn away from what we have done wrong and c) rejecting our own attempts to make ourselves right with God, freely accept Christ's forgiveness offered to us through faith. And that's all.

It's vital we realise that to put our trust in what we have done ourselves, whether by living what we might consider a good life or doing good things, is actually to reject that free gift. Imagine that the manager of a Michelin star restaurant with a world-famous chef invited you to a free meal. Would you consider bringing your sandwiches with you and putting them on the table? I think not. It would be an appalling insult! In the same way it's insulting to God to try to add anything to what he has done for us on the cross. In the words of a famous old hymn, 'Nothing in my hand I bring, simply to the cross I cling.'

SECOND, to accept Jesus as your Saviour is to enter into a relationship with him. Yes, God offers to freely pay off all the debts we have incurred with him because of our sin. But you and I cannot simply take God's pardon and walk away with never a second thought for how it was achieved or what we ought to do as a result. With our acceptance of God's free gift of forgiveness comes the commitment to a lifetime allegiance to Christ. In the culture of the Bible and many parts of the world today, to accept a gift is to accept an obligation: it is to take on a bond of loyalty between you and the one who offered you the gift. Salvation – being forgiven – is a free gift but in accepting it we make a commitment to follow Christ.

One way of thinking about what it means to accept Jesus' offer is to consider it as an opportunity to join his family. Because of a long tradition of individualism in much of Europe and North America we can overlook the significance of being in a family.

Yet, as I pointed out in the previous answer, the Bible talks a lot about the idea of adoption. To become a believer is to become a brother and sister of Christ and, with him, everybody else in the church. We become family. It's perhaps helpful here to think of a situation in which a difficult child from a deprived and troubled background is adopted into a loving and stable family of wealth and means. The expectation is that the child will adopt the values of his or her new family, will get rid of old habits and will slowly learn new and appropriate ways of thinking and acting.

To become a Christian is like that: it is to desire to conform more and more to the standard and pattern of life that Christ himself set out and which is portrayed for us in the gospels. Eventually, the hope is that we will display a genuine family likeness and be recognised as those who are indeed brothers and sisters of Jesus Christ.

To return to the question: to claim that we have trusted in Jesus but not to be trying to follow him suggests that you haven't really understood what God's forgiveness is all about. We need constantly to fight against those things that make us less like Christ and instead to desire those things that make us more like him. We are his family: let's live up to the standard he set.

# DO WE GET A SECOND OPPORTUNITY AFTER DEATH?

There's something incredibly attractive about the idea of a second opportunity; the possibility of, after having messed up an exam or an interview, being able to do it all over again. I imagine a good many of us would be walking or cycling to work if there had been no second (or third, fourth or fifth) opportunity on the driving test.

**BUT WHAT ABOUT LIFE?** Is there some post-mortem way of making up for our flawed lives with the wrong deeds that we have committed and good deeds we omitted? Now I am not referring to how God deals with those people who have never heard about Jesus and whether he offers them forgiveness and on what basis. No one knows what will happen to those who have never heard about that invitation, except we may be sure that it will involve Jesus and will be based on God's great principles of justice and mercy.

The idea of a 'second opportunity' I want to talk about applies to those who, despite having heard about Christ in this life, have deliberately chosen to reject him. They have rejected God's offer of forgiveness and have decided that, rather than accept Jesus as Saviour and Lord, they would rather run their lives on the all-too-common desire of 'I'm going to do it my way'.

Actually, it's difficult to know what people mean by 'a second opportunity'. I suspect that most people imagine it as operating on the same principle as those courses on the perils of speeding that you get offered to avoid points on your driving licence when you have been caught over the speed limit. It seems to be imagined that, after a few years of, at best, mild discomfort and, at worst, tolerable torment, your penalty points are lifted and, with your record wiped clean of offences, you are finally allowed access to heaven.

Well, while there are attractions to this idea of a second opportunity, I can't support it for several reasons. The first is because it flies in the face of what we know of how God saves people. If you believe that men and women are made right with God by 'doing good things', then I suppose it's possible to imagine that a few years of enduring some kind of punishment might make up for a misspent earthly life. But that is not how 'getting to heaven' works.

The only way any human being will ever be in heaven will be because Jesus died for them on the cross. Doing good things, in this life or the next, will not help anybody because the only way of being saved is to trust in Christ and accept him as the one who paid the price for our sins on the cross. If you want to go to heaven you have to go via King's Cross! That step of faith allows us to become new people, permanently cleansed from sin by Jesus. As the New Testament claims, 'the blood of Jesus, his Son, purifies us from all sin' (1 John 1:7). I don't see how any sort of 'second opportunity' involving individuals somehow paying off their own moral debts fits with this.

THE SECOND REASON that the idea of a 'second opportunity' is not something to hope for, is that there is no Bible evidence for it. The New Testament letter to the Hebrews is as clear as it can be: 'Just as people are destined to die once, and after that to face judgement . . .' (Hebrews 9:27).

Wherever the Bible talks about the future after death, it sees it simply in terms of heaven and hell. In the New Testament there is no hint of any kind of halfway house that would allow for a delayed entrance into heaven after an appropriate course of 'therapy'. The New Testament is consistent: the life we are living now – and this life only – is where we are either saved or lost for all eternity. Furthermore, nothing in the history of the early church indicates that they thought a second opportunity was possible. The urgency with which the first Christians surged around the Mediterranean telling everybody they could find to put their faith in Jesus, suggests no one had told them about a second opportunity.

A THIRD REASON is that I find this 'second opportunity' idea psychologically problematic. If someone has rejected Christ in this life it's difficult to see how a second opportunity is going to make much difference. With age, opinions become less fluid and more fixed. There's an old English saying based on Ecclesiastes 11:3 that runs like this:

As a tree falls, so shall it lie;
As a man lives, so shall he die;
As a man dies, so shall he be;
Through all the eons of eternity.

FINALLY, as an evangelist I have to say that I have my own reasons for rejecting this idea of a second opportunity. It removes the *need* to make a decision for Jesus because there is the idea that we can make it up after death. It also removes the *urgency* in making a decision for Jesus. It was a helpful image of older preachers that there was a 'gospel train' standing before you that you either caught or missed. To believe in a second opportunity is to stand on the platform with the gospel train carriage doors open wide before you and to step back from it saying, 'Actually, I think I'm going to wait for the next train.' Let me be honest: everything I know tells me that to do this is a terrible mistake. There is no 'next train'.

I should also say here that not only do I reject the idea of a second opportunity but I also reject the concept that is often linked with it, of praying for those who have died. Emotionally, I understand why people do this, but I don't think it's helpful. If there are only two states after death, then those in heaven don't need our prayers while those in 'the other place' are beyond the help of prayer. Sadly, we must commit the dead to the mercy of God and move on with our own lives.

Let me conclude by reminding you that we shouldn't prejudge people's eternal state. Who knows what goes on as someone comes close to death and indeed starts to go into the process of dying? The account of the thief on the cross (Luke 23:39–43) is very encouraging. Here, in the last hours of his life, we see a very bad man finding forgiveness from Jesus and being promised immediate access to heaven. Deathbed conversions do occur but please don't leave it till then. There are some things in life too important to risk and eternity is most definitely one of them. Don't rely on a second opportunity. When it comes to the next life, this life is the only life that counts.

# DO ALL RELIGIONS LEAD TO GOD?

In our modern climate of thinking where nothing is truly wrong except to say that something *is* wrong, a part of me would love to be able to say 'yes' to the idea that all religions lead to God. It would be very convenient to announce with a big smile that all religions and philosophies are equally valuable aspects of some greater underlying cosmic reality. I'd also have a lot more holidays to celebrate. I suspect I'm not alone here: most of us like to make and keep friends and we hate saying those uncomfortable words, 'I'm sorry, I don't agree with that.' Yet the fact is that here, as in every area of life from Architecture to Zoology, not every answer is correct and we need to find out what exactly is true.

In any discussion on different religions, we have to come to terms with the unarguable fact that Jesus made such extraordinary claims about his relationship to God that he placed himself in a unique position. Perhaps the most famous is his claim, 'I am the way and the truth and the life. No one comes to the Father except through me' (John 14:6). Yet this verse does not stand alone; all the way through his ministry Jesus claimed both a relationship to God and offered access to God in a way that is both unique and exclusive. Certainly, the idea that God can only be found through Jesus was the view of the first Christians (see, for example, Acts 4:12, 'Salvation is found in no one else, for there is no other name under heaven given to mankind by which we must be saved').

So, how are we to view other religions? I think the best way of looking at this is to consider three separate questions.

THE FIRST QUESTION is *Who is God?* Atheism says that there is no God, Buddhism is unclear about God, Hinduism believes in many gods, Judaism and Islam believe that there is just one God and Christianity believes in one God who is three persons. It seems obvious that while these views might all be wrong, they can't all be right. Matters are even more complicated because the qualities and characters of these various gods are also very different. In some cases God is a person, while in other cases he is more like a force. In some religions that think of God in personal terms, it's not really worth bothering with whoever is in charge up there because whether they are considered he, she, it or they, the fact is that they aren't 'interested in a relationship' with us. Christianity, in contrast, says that not only is God personal but that he loves the human race so much that he died for us. Because different religions give such varying views of who God is, it's hard to see how they can lead the same way. The destinations they point to look very different.

THE SECOND QUESTION asks *What is the problem between us and God?* Some religions seem to consider men and women to be basically good and decent beings whose only lack is knowledge and who merely need 'enlightenment'. Other religions see us as slightly flawed individuals, guilty of a mere naughtiness that God can easily overlook. Christianity takes a more sombre view. The Bible teaches that we are in serious trouble: we are not merely moral underachievers, we are those who have rebelled against a holy God and as a result are in trouble. Again, with totally different diagnoses of the human condition, it's hard to see how all religions point the same way.

THE THIRD QUESTION – and it is one that exposes major differences between Christianity and other faiths – is *How do we meet God?* Most religions talk about men and women seeking God and a common image is of the individual climbing up some mountain peak of morality or spirituality to try to get closer to the divine being who is there on the summit. Christianity, however, has a very different perspective. With the bad news that human beings cannot ascend to God comes the good news that he has come down to us instead. God came to the human race partially in the words of the Old Testament prophets and then, finally and fully, in human form as Jesus of Nazareth. The result of this is the paradox that although Christianity teaches the biggest and severest gap between human beings and God, it offers the greatest hope because it says that this chasm has been bridged by Christ himself. Precisely because we cannot save ourselves, God has come to earth in Christ to save us. Once more, we see that different religions point not in the same direction but in totally different ones.

For the Christian this gives a fresh perspective on other religions: the fundamental problem is not so much that other faiths are wrong, but that they do not deal with the severity of the human problem. When what we need is drastic surgery, all they can offer is bandages.

So let's return to the original question: do all religions lead to God? Let me offer you an image which I hope will help. Imagine that at the heart of some ancient country, unenlightened by any notions of democracy or lenient punishment, there exists an extraordinarily solemn and daunting building that is the court of law. Those individuals who have been accused of crimes enter its front door and are led, trembling with fear, deep into a stark and intimidating courtroom where they stand awaiting a judgement of jail or death. After an intimidating ceremony, a severe judge dressed in imposing robes enters and takes his seat high above the accused. From there, without any trace of mercy or hesitation, the judge solemnly proceeds to pass firm sentences on the accused individuals.

Eventually, with the court emptied of prisoners, the judge retires to his chambers. Now imagine that there is a backdoor to this monumental court of law and through it a small child enters and is ushered through to the judge's chambers where, his robes now hanging on the wall, the judge sits at ease in a chair. The infant runs over to him and, with the warmest and softest of smiles, the judge stands up, bends down and picks up the child. 'Daddy!' the infant cries with delight, feeling the gentle embrace. 'My child!' responds the judge with warm affection.

It seems to me that this image is helpful. In one way, whichever road of life we take will ultimately bring us to meet God. That appointment between us and him is indelibly marked on God's calendar, if not ours. But – and here's the infinitely important question – on what basis will that encounter be? Will we meet him as the guilty party before a judge in a court room or will we meet him as our loving father in a family meeting? It's the most profound of differences. Only the Christian faith gives us the privilege and security of coming to God as his child. That's the difference Jesus makes!

# WHAT SHOULD I DO IF I LIKE JESUS BUT I DON'T LIKE CHRISTIANS?

When faced with some questions the only sensible response is another question and here the obvious one is 'What *exactly* is it about Christians that you don't like?' The reality is that there are various reasons why someone may say 'I don't like Christians'.

**THE FIRST REASON** may simply be because the individual concerned has encountered some Christians with whom they do not feel socially or culturally comfortable. They are individuals who 'don't talk my language', 'aren't my sort of people', 'read the wrong newspapers' or even have 'dreadful dress sense'. Well, I make no apology for this; the reality is that those who come to faith in Christ are an extraordinarily mixed bunch. It's not uncommon for any reasonably sized church to include professors, lawyers and surgeons as well as cleaners, refugees and those who struggle to read. While some people may find this range of individuals somewhat awkward, it is in fact the joy of the church. God did not intend to create a social club with rigid rules about who may belong, but instead a family whose only entry requirement is the recognition that, in Jesus, God has answered our deepest needs.

That the doors of the church are thrown wide to all is a principle that was established by Jesus. He went out of his way to select as disciples those whose distinguishing feature was that they were undistinguished. He also acquired disciples who were extraordinarily varied: in Jericho alone we read how Jesus acquired as followers a chief tax collector (Luke 19:1–10) and a beggar healed from blindness (Mark 10:46–52).

The same principle of outrageous and almost offensive inclusivity operated in the early church. Paul, writing to the church in Corinth, reminded them that 'not many of you were wise by human standards; not many were influential; not many were of noble birth. But God chose the foolish things of the world to shame the wise; God chose the weak things of the world to shame the strong' (1 Corinthians 1:26–27).

That principle has not changed. Mind you, if you choose to follow a disgraced and executed Jewish carpenter, you shouldn't be too surprised if you find yourself in rather strange company.

A SECOND OBJECTION some people may have to Christians is that they find their behaviour odd and even uncomfortable. Perhaps it's the way they smile during services, wave their arms about during songs, or feel 'led to pray for you'. Actually, such things are really only 'trivially' odd. If Christians were consistent with their own beliefs they *should*, by definition, be 'seriously' odd. After all, to become a Christian is to realise that there are new dimensions in life and you are now living with a totally new and radical set of priorities and perspectives. Whereas before, your rule of behaviour might have been 'Is this action going to bring me pleasure or regret?' your new rule is very different: 'Is this right and pleasing to God?' And, by this world's standards, that's *seriously* odd.

Precisely because to become a Christian is to be under entirely new operating instructions, you could in fact argue that one of the problems with the modern church is that Christians are not even odder.

All the evidence from the secular authors of the first couple of centuries AD is that the first followers of Jesus were considered a nuisance because they totally failed to fit in with Roman culture: they didn't engage in sexual immorality, didn't worship Caesar and they had an embarrassingly high level of social care for one another. They were people who were marching to the beat of a very different drum and that troubled their contemporaries. Church history tells us how this story has been repeated: when the followers of Jesus stand up for his values, they can suddenly find themselves very unpopular indeed.

Actually, although I've often heard many criticisms of Christians on superficial or cultural matters, it's this moral dimension that really hurts. If you're quietly fiddling your travel expenses ('everyone does it!') it's not good news to have some convert announce that she's handed back the money that she took. If you're engaged in an extramarital affair then you really aren't going to welcome hearing a man say how God saved his marriage after he repented of his infidelities. Goodness and holiness – and those who practise them – may be nice ideas in theory but in reality and up close they can be very uncomfortable. It's worth remembering that a lot of people were anxious to try to get Jesus out of the way!

Now, if 'What should I do if I like Jesus but I don't like Christians?' is your question, let me propose four answers.

FIRST, remember that you are called to believe and trust in Christ, not his followers.

SECOND, if you struggle with the idea of getting alongside Christians and belonging with them in a church, then think of it as being your tiny and distinctly inadequate response to what Jesus did for you. If he got tortured and nailed to the cross, you can at least put up with some awkward people for a few hours once a week.

THIRD, the process of getting alongside those who you wouldn't naturally want to get alongside may actually be beneficial for you. Quite frequently, God uses other Christians to do good to us; after all, being pushed against abrasive material is an excellent way to have the rough edges of anything, including human lives, smoothed off.

**AND FINALLY**, always remember that although you may find dealing with the followers of Jesus difficult, it may also be that they feel the same about you.

# PART FIVE

# LIFE AFTER LIFE: THE FUTURE, HEAVEN AND HELL

There is, to coin a phrase, a paradox about paradise. Actually, there's a pair of them. The first is that Christians, for whom paradise – life after death – is something that should be central to their lives, often seem awkward talking about it. The second is that the noisy enemies of Christianity delight in ridiculing the idea of the afterlife despite the fact that one of their biggest issues is that they have nothing at all to offer in its place.

Indeed, one of the big problems – perhaps *the* biggest problem – of atheism is quite simply that it offers no hope whatsoever for any sort of survival beyond death. In making that depressing claim, atheism doesn't simply rob the future of hope, it robs the present of meaning. After all, what is the point of writing that great book, painting that wonderful picture or ending poverty for millions if all that we manage to achieve ends with our death? According to atheism, the main point about life is that it's pointless.

It seems to me undeniable that in modern Christianity there is a widespread hesitancy in talking about the afterlife. So I make no apology for having six questions about heaven and – on the principle of keeping a satisfactory balance – one about hell.

# CAN WE BE RAISED FROM THE DEAD IF WE ARE CREMATED?

The way that cremation turns a recognisable human body into a small pile of grey ash is disconcerting and it's hardly surprising that it raises questions, not least when faced with the Christian claim that God can, and will, reverse the process.

Let's give some background to this. In the Old Testament there was the belief that, one day, the dead would be physically raised, given new bodies and judged by God (Job 19:25–27; Daniel 12:2). The first Christians agreed with this but saw it as occurring at the return of Jesus (for example, John 5:28–29; 1 Corinthians 15:52; 1 Thessalonians 4:16). These believers didn't just base their ideas about what would happen after death simply on Jesus' teaching but also on his resurrection. That was an event which they saw as the prototype of the resurrection that would, one day, occur to all (1 Corinthians 15:22–23; Philippians 3:20–21). Despite the views of many people who, influenced by Greek philosophy, saw the afterlife simply as some sort of spiritual event, Christians – following their Jewish ancestors – believed in a very solid and very physical resurrection of flesh and bones.

This idea of a physical resurrection of the dead is sometimes used by critics as an argument against Christianity. They assume that the first believers had some naïve idea of God finding their buried skeletons, sticking the bones back together and then putting flesh on them. Given that, they say, how is any sort of resurrection possible when all you have is a few handfuls of ash?

A moment's thought will tell you that thinking believers must always have realised it was never quite that simple. They would have known people who had been burnt to powder in flames or been completely digested by wild animals. After all, in the first century there was no shortage of good Christians who had been reduced to charcoal at the stake or had been last glimpsed disappearing down the digestive tract of some lion in the amphitheatre.

Yet it's an intriguing question and let me make it even tougher. On 6th August 1945 the United States dropped an atom bomb on Hiroshima and then, three days later, another on Nagasaki. In total over 200,000 people were killed and at the centre of the explosions any individuals present were instantly vaporised, not simply into atoms but into sub-atomic particles. Given that Nagasaki was the centre of Christianity in Japan, one presumes this fate happened to many believers in Jesus.

So how can God possibly bring back into physical existence bodies that have long since disintegrated into dust? Here, as so often when we think about the afterlife, we can only speculate and so *cautiously* I offer two suggestions that may help.

FIRST, if you have a smartphone or know how they work, you are probably aware that in most cases, even if they are packed full of data, losing or smashing one is not an utter disaster. If you have been wise, your data will have been 'backed up in the cloud'. Now, although I would struggle to explain how that works, I do know that if I have to get a replacement phone, I simply log into the appropriate account and press 'Restore' and in a way that seems miraculous to me, my precious data floods back onto the new phone so that it becomes, in effect, a resurrected version of my old phone.

Given that God is seriously smarter than the smartest smartphone, isn't it possible that what we are in terms of body, mind and spirit are 'backed up' with him? If so, then at the return of Christ, all that is needed for God to do is issue that command *'Restore!'* I don't see why not.

A SECOND way of thinking about the resurrection of the dead centres on the fact, touched on earlier, that throughout the Bible, God describes himself in language that suggests he is not just eternal but somehow outside time. For instance, he calls himself 'Yahweh' when he reveals himself to Moses (Exodus 3:14), a name which can be translated as

'I am who I am' – not 'I was' or 'I will be' but '*I am*' – and with that comes the idea that God is someone who is in some way beyond past, present and future. The idea that God is eternal or 'from everlasting to everlasting' in the sense of being completely beyond time is found in many Bible verses (see, for example, Psalm 90:2; Isaiah 57:15; Jude 25).

From such a vantage point outside and beyond days and years, God can see all our lives, from the moment of our birth in the past to the moment when, sometime in the future, we die. I find the idea that God has the life of everybody who has ever existed (and still to exist) before him very helpful. It would surely mean that if he wanted to make a 'new version' of someone who died years ago, he could simply refer to their whole existence stretched out in front of him, choose some particularly suitable moment and then restore them to life from that.

Both of these suggestions may be too simple, but they demonstrate that it is perfectly possible to imagine ways in which an all-powerful and all-wise God could recreate us in the future, whatever has happened to our bodies in the meantime.

Ultimately, how God will raise our bodies to some future state is not the most important question for us. What should be of far greater concern is *where* those immortal bodies are going to spend eternity.

# WILL WE RECOGNISE FAMILY AND FRIENDS IN HEAVEN?

One of the most common questions about heaven is whether or not we will recognise family and friends there. This is often a deeply emotional and heartfelt question coming perhaps from a parent who has lost a child or from those who, having been happily married for decades, now find themselves alone. It's a question where, while holding to the truth, we need to be sensitive.

I feel that we have enough evidence from the Bible to give a 'yes' answer to this question but it's an answer that needs thinking through carefully. At the start, I would suggest that we must hold onto three general principles.

**THE FIRST PRINCIPLE** is that the focus of heaven is God, not us. I'm afraid you sometimes hear people talk about heaven as if its purpose was nothing more than to provide an opportunity for the biggest and longest family reunion ever. Actually, the Bible makes it clear that heaven is far more than the gathering together of long-separated relatives and friends; it is about being present with God as he truly is for eternity.

The purpose of heaven is something repeatedly shown in the book of Revelation (consider chapters 4 and 5; 7:9–12; 11:15–18; 15:2–4; 19:1–8; 22:3–5). In heaven, the centre of attention will be the Christ who saved us, not our family or friends. That is not to say there won't be opportunity for reunions as well; by any reckoning eternity is a very long time.

THE SECOND PRINCIPLE is that heaven is going to be superior to this world in every way. So we are told that there will be no marriage in heaven (Luke 20:34–36). Although this may sound like a loss, Christian thinkers have long presumed that it is not because heaven limits our pleasures but, on the contrary, because there will be better and richer relationships in heaven than even in the best marriage. After all, one of the characteristics of a marriage on earth is that it is necessarily exclusive and the emotional and psychological intimacy it offers can be enjoyed by the husband and wife alone. It's been imagined that one of the characteristics of heaven is that we will be able to have deep emotional and psychological relationships, not just with a single spouse, but with countless numbers of people.

THE THIRD PRINCIPLE is that heaven is the place of healing. It is the place where justice is done, where losses are made good, where sorrows are ended and where all that can be put right will be put right (Revelation 21:3–5).

Let me – again cautiously – add some thoughts to these broad principles.

- The references in the Bible to the afterlife or to heaven often involve a restoration of relationships. The Old Testament talks about people being 'gathered to their ancestors' (see Genesis 25:17; 35:29; 49:33) and David anticipates being reunited with his son (2 Samuel 12:23). It is clear in the New Testament that the destiny of all who follow Jesus is to be with him in heaven (for example, Luke 23:43; 2 Corinthians 5:8). Paul reassures grieving believers in Thessalonica that, when Christ returns, both the dead and the living will 'be caught up . . . to meet the Lord in the air. And so we will be with the Lord forever' (1 Thessalonians 4:17). From these verses we can conclude that in heaven individuals will be able to recognise and relate to each other.

- Nevertheless, it is clear that those who are in heaven will not be exactly who they were. As the resurrected Jesus was changed, so those who follow him will also be changed (see 1 Corinthians 15:49, 53). Those changes will, I presume, be not just physical but also spiritual and psychological (1 Corinthians 13:12). So although you may have known someone as having an anxious and slightly depressed personality, that is surely not how they will be in heaven; after all, we are promised unlimited joy (2 Corinthians 4:17; Revelation 7:13–17; 19:1–10). Although we will not be angels, I suspect if we could see ourselves as we will be, we would probably imagine we were seeing angels.

- Despite these changes of healing and 'glorification' our personal identity – who we are – will persist into heaven. Jesus is very clear that he will meet his followers in heaven (see Matthew 26:29 and John 14:3).

So I think in heaven we will know each other and be known. Yet it's important to remember that heaven is not just going to be us on our own; it's going to be a vast community centred on Christ 'from every tribe and language and people and nation' (Revelation 5:9; see also Luke 13:29; Revelation 19:1–6). And bearing in mind those images of wedding feasts and banquets (Isaiah 25:6; Matthew 8:11–12; 22:3–10; Revelation 19:9) there is going to be joyful fellowship, not just with those from our past but with everyone else from different cultures and ages. There will be old friends there, endless new ones and, most of all, Christ.

# WILL I BE FAT IN HEAVEN?

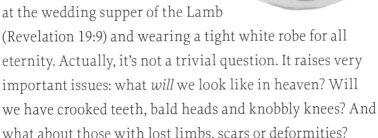

Some of us who struggle with our waistlines have concerns that we will still be overweight in heaven. We are worried about having to choose the low-calorie option at the wedding supper of the Lamb (Revelation 19:9) and wearing a tight white robe for all eternity. Actually, it's not a trivial question. It raises very important issues: what *will* we look like in heaven? Will we have crooked teeth, bald heads and knobbly knees? And what about those with lost limbs, scars or deformities?

These are important and sensitive issues, but they are also tricky ones. The Bible talks a lot about believers being raised from the dead and going to be 'with the Lord' forever but it offers us few details. Our best information comes from the descriptions of Jesus after the resurrection and from teaching in the letters, especially by Paul in 1 Corinthians 15. Given our limited data, the safest answer to most questions to do with heaven is simply 'we don't know'. Nevertheless, some things *can* be said and let me suggest five certainties that I find in the Bible that are helpful.

**FIRST**, heaven is going to be a joyful place of fulfilment and perfection where we who have followed Christ will experience the full presence of God and spend an eternity safe from any form of anxiety, pain, grief, suffering or evil. And 'evil' includes fear, shame, disgust and self-loathing.

**SECOND**, heaven is a real, solid place and we who, thanks to Jesus, get there are going to be equally real and solid. Any idea of faint, transparent spirits holding harps and sitting on fluffy clouds should be ignored. In heaven we will have bodies that are more solid than those we have at the moment.

**THIRD**, in heaven we will be very different to what we are now; as different, Paul says, as a seed and the plant or tree that it grows into (1 Corinthians 15:36–37). That extraordinary change may explain why we are told so little about the resurrection body: it would be hard to explain to a tadpole what it's like to jump like a frog, or to a caterpillar what it's like to fly like a butterfly.

**FOURTH**, our new bodies will be perfect and glorious. Now although that's an idea that greatly appeals to me when I look in the mirror, step on the scales or go to the doctor, neither I, nor anybody else, knows exactly what that means. Nevertheless, what we will have will be a definite improvement on the disintegrating bodies we have now. Those of us who follow Christ are not going to merely get some cosmetic makeover, but a whole-body upgrade!

**FIFTH**, despite this extraordinary change we will, however, keep our identity in heaven. If you have put your faith in Jesus, then it is *you* personally who will be in heaven. The disciples were in no doubt that the Jesus who met with them after the resurrection was the same man they had followed for three years. The same principle will apply in heaven: despite our upgraded bodies you will still be you and I will still be me.

Because heaven is a place of perfection, I think we will each have a perfect body in shape and size. We definitely won't be visiting Weight Watchers! We will be whole and healthy, no pains, aches, no diseases and with 20:20 vision as there will be so much to see.

Will I be fat in heaven? No! I will be happy and content with everything.

# IN HEAVEN, WILL WE KNOW WHAT WE DID ON EARTH?

think that there are strong reasons to suggest that in heaven we will remember the past, but I would want to add a qualifying comment: *at least to some degree.* Some people deny that we will remember anything in heaven on the basis of Isaiah 65:17, 'I will create new heavens and a new earth. The former things will not be remembered, nor will they come to mind.' Along with many commentators, I think this isn't a universal rule but something that only applies to specific 'former things' in Israel's history. I think, as a general principle, there will be at least a selective memory in heaven and let me justify this with two reasons.

**THE FIRST REASON** is that our memories are part of who we are: they link us to our past. If my memory is erased, in what sense am *I* still *me*? Equally, if we are going to be able to recognise family and friends, we will need to recognise them in the context of what we and they did together. Somehow the expression 'Don't I remember you from somewhere?' seems rather inappropriate for heaven. Without memories, an identity is simply a nametag and

virtually meaningless. In fact, I think one of the joys
of heaven for those who have suffered dementia and
Alzheimer's (and for the rest of us who have merely forgotten
more than we can remember) will be the recovery of memory.
Now because not all memories are pleasant (indeed some
are horrific) and we all have recollections that deeply hurt
and embarrass us, I think that we will revisit our past from
heaven's perspective but nothing bad from earth will enter
heaven – it's as if every bad memory will be filtered out.
As our bodies will be healed and transformed, so will our
memories be.

**A SECOND REASON** why those in heaven will retain their
memories is that much of what is done in heaven will centre
on thanksgiving and praise (for example, Revelation 15:3).
What will we give thanks for if we have no memories?
Surely a key element in giving thanks in eternity will be
the way that, from the standpoint of the new and eternal
Jerusalem, we can look back on our lives and see what
happened from God's perspective. We will be able to revisit
our lives and see such moments where, invisible to us, God
miraculously kept us from temptation; where, in what we
took to be merely advice from a friend, God spoke guidance
to us; and where unseen angels prevented us from some
appalling fate.

There will be much to thank God for in the remembering
of our past lives. Yet although we can only speculate how,
it seems certain that heaven will be an active place and,

as eternity progresses, the new creation will bring new activities and responsibilities. Ultimately, I expect many of the memories of this life will be replaced by those wonders that we become involved in there. But I suspect we will never forget why we are there: because Jesus saved us out of love.

# DO BABIES GO TO HEAVEN WHEN THEY DIE?

First of all, if this is not a question you've ever asked, be *very* grateful. There was a time when this question was widely discussed because almost every family had one or more infants who had died. In the nineteenth century nearly a quarter of infants in poor areas of Britain died before they were one year old. I'm afraid to say there are still many parts of the world where death rates amongst children are appallingly high. Here are some chilling figures: in 2016, it was estimated that across the globe 5.6 million children under the age of five died in the course of the year; that's 15,000 every day. I don't think things have improved since.

Although whether infants go to heaven is not a topic treated by the Bible, along with most Christians throughout history I believe that they do. Nevertheless, I need to justify that answer. There is always a danger of wishful thinking and it's worth remembering that just because we would like something to be true, does not make it true.

Some people say that babies go to heaven simply because they are 'innocent'. Actually, here the Bible disagrees.

It clearly implies that the entire human race, from our earliest days, choose wrong over right. So, for instance, in Psalm 51:5 we read David's confession: 'Surely I was sinful at birth, sinful from the time my mother conceived me.' Paul writes these uncomfortable words in Ephesians 2:3: 'All of us also lived among them at one time, gratifying the cravings of our flesh and following its desires and thoughts. Like the rest, we were by nature deserving of wrath.' That babies are not innocent is the testimony of anyone with any experience of them: not only do even the youngest infants seem to have a sense of what is right or wrong, but they seem to be quite happy being disobedient and choosing the wrong over the right.

So on what basis is there hope for infants? I think there are three lines of evidence that infants who die do go to heaven.

THE FIRST involves the fundamental moral principle that if you don't know a rule, you can't be judged by it. This is clearly stated in the Bible. So, for example, Jesus, once arguing with the Pharisees (the leaders of God's people), accused them of being spiritually blind. When they denied this, Jesus said, 'If you were blind, you would not be guilty of sin; but now that you claim you can see, your guilt remains' (John 9:41). Paul says something similar in Romans 5:13: 'To be sure, sin was in the world before the law was given, but sin is not charged against anyone's account where there is no law.' Here, ignorance is innocence.

THE SECOND line of evidence comes from the sad story of King David and his adultery with Bathsheba. The boy that was born out of this act became sick and eventually died. In referring to his death, the grieving king comforted himself by saying, 'I will go to him, but he will not return to me' (2 Samuel 12:23). This strongly suggests that he knew the child would be waiting for him in the afterlife.

A FINAL line of evidence is quite simply the love that was shown by Jesus for children. In a culture that marginalised and ignored infants, Jesus cared for them and treated them as having value (Matthew 18:1–5; 19:13–15; Mark 10:13–16; Luke 18:15–17). The idea that children would not go to heaven seems utterly inconsistent with Jesus' concern for them.

So my view is that every child who dies in infancy and who has not had an opportunity of making an informed choice to accept or reject Christ, will be in heaven. I would extend that view to those who have such mental problems that they remain, in effect, childlike throughout their lives. And I believe that every aborted baby and miscarriage is in heaven.

Let me make two final observations.

THE FIRST is that this positive view of a child's status before God should not minimise the responsibility of teaching them about Jesus and encouraging them to make a decision as early as possible to love him. I know of many Christians who trace their faith to decisions made when they were four or five.

**THE SECOND** is to raise another question to which I can only give a very cautious answer: if babies go to heaven do they stay as babies there? I think that heaven is not just where sorrows are ended and where wrong is mended but it is also a place where the frustrations and failures of this life are resolved. On that basis I think it perfectly likely that, in heaven, babies become not what they were but what they might have been. But the great thing about God is that we can be sure that, in Christ, things will be better than we can imagine.

# WILL I WEAR CLOTHES IN HEAVEN?

To be absolutely honest, what we are going to wear in heaven is not a question that has ever worried me. After all, it's not as though you can pack clothes for the trip. Nevertheless, like many other seemingly trivial questions it does raise some interesting points. So, for instance, I gather there are some who think that because Adam and Eve were originally naked, the inhabitants of heaven – the new paradise – will also be naked. As far as I am aware most artists who have tried to paint heaven have, rather understandably, failed to incorporate this concept in their paintings. Personally,

I'm very negative about the concept of paradise as an eternal naturist park. For a start, we can safely assume the resurrected Jesus wore clothes. After all, it's difficult to see how, had he been stark naked, Mary Magdalene would have stood around long to talk with him (John 20:14–15) or that the two disciples on the way to Emmaus would have welcomed his company (Luke 24:13–35).

Two other possibilities have been raised. One is that we will be dressed for eternity in the clothes we are buried in. Given that you rarely get to choose what you are buried in, that some people are eaten by sharks while in their swimming costumes and that many people are only ever buried in rags, I'm unconvinced. I'm equally negative about a heaven in which we are all wearing peasant robes or togas in a style last fashionable in Galilee AD 30 or Corinth AD 50. Actually, given the wedding imagery so widely used of heaven it seems to me likely that we will wear the finest clothing, whether of our age or of another age. We will be dressed up as we have never been (Matthew 22:11–12).

There are some easily overlooked but relevant and very interesting comments in Revelation 21. Talking of the New Jerusalem we read in verse 24, 'The nations will walk by its light, and the kings of the earth will bring their splendour into it', and in verse 26, 'The glory and honour of the nations will be brought into it'. I'm reminded here of Jesus pointing to the 'lilies of the field' and saying, 'Yet I tell you that not even Solomon in all his splendour was dressed like one of these'

(Matthew 6:29). Clothes can be splendid and the clothes of a monarch are particularly splendid: why should those brothers and sisters of the King of kings not have the most glorious of garments to wear?

If I'm not entirely sure *what* we wear, I can say something about *how* we will wear clothes. You see, sometimes in this life people wear clothes to attract other people, to hide who they really are, to intimidate others or even to boast how rich they are. None of those reasons will exist in heaven. What we wear in heaven will be worn for the very best reasons: we will be celebrating. There will be a lot to celebrate.

# DOES HELL EXIST AND IF IT DOES WHAT'S THE POINT OF IT?

Trust me, I really wish I didn't believe that hell exists, but I do. Jesus mentions hell a lot (for example, Matthew 8:12; 10:28; 25:46; Luke 16:19–31; John 5:29). If Jesus was wrong about hell, then why should we believe him about heaven? It's certainly a subject I would prefer not to talk about. I like to be enthusiastic and no one with any sensitivity can treat the idea of hell with enthusiasm. But we can't ignore something just because we don't like it.

So, if hell exists, what is it like? A curious fact is that most of the ideas we have about hell don't come from the Bible (the only reliable source) and much of the language there ('fire', 'darkness', 'undying worms') is surely symbolic. Nevertheless, this sort of imagery expresses an unimaginable reality: a horrible, terrifying condition that can neither be mended nor ended.

As with everything else to do with what happens beyond this life, we must be careful to distinguish certainty from speculation but one idea that has helped many people understand hell is that it is a place or situation *where God is not*. If we accept that God is the source of every good thing and God is not present in hell then there can be nothing good there: no hope, no peace, no rest, no forgiveness. Hell is every bad thing that you can think of without anything good to compensate. Some people joke about there being better company in hell: I'm afraid friendship or companionship is going to be one of those things that is not possible.

If hell is indeed to do with the *absence* of God and anything good, some people have suggested that in contrast to a heaven which grows and expands eternally in glory, hell progressively declines into an empty point of nothingness. Perhaps. Whether hell is truly unending or whether, at some point, it and its inhabitants cease to exist is much debated amongst Christians. Even if hell were to be for a limited period before the total extinction of existence, it remains a terrible and appalling fate.

What's the point of hell? I think there are two reasons why hell exists and they balance each other. The first reason is the justice of God. Hell is a place of judgement: here, sentence is passed on those who have rejected God's extraordinary offer of forgiveness through repentance and faith in Jesus. The fact that we have all fallen short of God's standards means that hell is the 'default destination' for all human beings. The Bible implies that this principle of justice means that there will be greater and lesser punishments in hell (see Matthew 11:20–24; Luke 12:42–48). I would imagine that precisely because hell is based on justice, no one who ends up there will ever be able to protest that their fate is unfair and undeserved.

This idea of hell as the place of final justice is significant because all of us, whether Christians or not, want there to be some sort of ultimate accounting. The thought that someone could live a life of cheating, bullying and violence without ever facing any sort of reckoning is something that almost everybody finds objectionable. This deep-felt universal hunger for justice is why revenge is such a major theme in films and books. While we may want mercy for ourselves and our loved ones, deep within us all lies the hope that one day, justice will finally be done. Hell is that place. Incidentally, do remember the distinct difference between hell and heaven. In hell, God's enemies get what they deserve; in heaven, God's friends are given freely what they do not deserve.

If the first reason for hell is God's justice, then the second reason is God's respect for human beings. Along with many other people, I believe that God respects human beings enough not to force himself on them. So, if someone totally refuses to accept God and wants to have nothing to do with him for ever, then I think it's quite possible that God is forced to give them what they want and allow them to go to the only place where he is not present. It sounds cruel but what else is God supposed to do?

If hell is so horrible, it may be asked, why doesn't God do something about it? The answer is, of course, that he *has* done all he can do about it: he came to earth in Jesus to die and to take on himself the horrors of hell for those who put their trust in him. Along with Christians throughout the ages I find the idea that Jesus has paid the price for our wrongdoing an enormous relief. As justice is so important to God, he cannot ask for payment to be made twice. In Christ, God has offered us a way out from this most appalling of fates: let's take it, but not because we don't want to go to hell, but because we want to go to heaven because God is there.

# PART SIX

# THE CHURCH AND LIVING AS GOD'S PEOPLE

There are an endless number of possible questions about the Christian life. Why are there so many denominations? Should Christians ever fight? Should we get involved in politics or protests? What do we do about global poverty? Is it wrong to spend a lot of money on clothes? Out of these infinite possibilities I have chosen just seven questions to answer. The reason for choosing these topics is partly because they interest me but also because they are varied and require different ways of responding.

The fact that these questions require different types of answers is important. To make what ought to be an obvious point, it is not enough to go back to the Bible and try to find in its pages rigid rulings on how we are to live. Unsurprisingly, the Bible gives little guidance on such things as organ transplants or the morality of the Internet. Yet that does not mean that when we are faced with a moral issue we have nothing to say. When Jesus was asked what was the greatest commandment in the Law, the answer he gave was probably more than his questioner bargained for. 'Jesus replied, "'Love the Lord your God with all your heart and with all your soul and with all your mind.' This is the first and greatest commandment. And the second is like it: 'Love your neighbour as yourself.' All the Law and the Prophets hang on these two commandments'" (Matthew 22:37–40).

Many books have been written on this answer, but I simply want to note the command we are given to love God *with our mind*. In other words, God expects us to think through issues prayerfully and carefully and by listening to the Holy Spirit. But thought is required.

So let's look at seven questions and my hope is that the responses will do more than answer these specific questions; they will also prompt you into ways of thinking about those many questions that I have not touched on.

# ISN'T THE CHURCH
# FULL OF HYPOCRITES?

It's a widespread accusation that the church is full of hypocrites: individuals whose private lives are very much inferior to how they present themselves in public. Of course, claims of hypocrisy are not confined to church circles. The accusation of being a hypocrite is a vice that anybody, especially a politician or public figure, risks. So, for example, it's common to read criticism of some celebrity who, having spoken out for 'green values' has been seen travelling by private jet. The word hypocrite comes from the Greek *hypocrisis* where it was used for a play actor, and that's why we don't like hypocrisy: it's an act.

Yet what people call hypocrisy is far more complicated and varied than we tend to think. There is what might be termed a 'deep hypocrisy': the situation where someone deliberately and cynically pretends to be decent, moral or even godly in order to obtain influence or make money. This involves deliberate deception and lying; it may be criminal and it certainly deserves every criticism. Cases do occur in churches (as in all other areas of public life) but I think they are rarer than many people imagine.

It's just that because this sort of deep hypocrisy is so scandalous, when it's exposed it makes the headlines.

What I suspect is far more common is something far milder. This is an accidental and possibly unrecognised gap between belief and behaviour. So, for instance, you could imagine the sad case where someone decides to become a Christian and becomes involved in church life, only to lose their spiritual passion and enthusiasm in subsequent years. The result may be that while they are still going through the 'motions of belief' a disconnect has grown up between what they stand for on a Sunday and how they behave at home or at work. The Christian faith is something that requires we have a living relationship with Jesus and if that lapses then a mismatch between the standards we profess and those we practise are more or less inevitable.

I think, however, we need to be aware that what is often considered hypocrisy is something rather different. This is a situation where people set up moral standards and try to live up to them but, somehow, they fail in their efforts. These people – 'moral underachievers' if you like – are those who have fallen short of their aspirations.

Now, I have to say I have some sympathies here. As I have noted in the next question, a genuine church is not full of perfect people. It is made up of those who recognise God's standards, try to live up to them but who, almost inevitably, fail to do so and find themselves seeking God's forgiveness.

Unless such people pretend that they haven't fallen short then they are hardly hypocrites.

This sort of gap between aspiration and reality is actually inevitable in churches. After all, the higher you set your moral standards, the easier it is to fall short of them and our standard is the highest: Jesus Christ. In fact, as Saint Paul recounts in chapter seven of his letter to the Romans, even he found that he failed to live up to the standards he held to. It is precisely because churches and Christians hold out moral standards that they are vulnerable to the charge of hypocrisy. After all, the safest remedy against being accused of hypocrisy is to avoid any claim to be moral. So, if you don't believe that being faithful to your spouse is something to value, you can hardly be accused of hypocrisy when you are found in bed with someone else.

This leads to two very curious but significant phenomena that I think only Christianity explains. The first is that all human beings, whether they are religious or not, set themselves some sort of moral standard to live by. It may be pretty minimal – 'I'm loyal to my friends' or 'I keep my promises' – but it's a standard. The second curious fact is that whatever standard we set – and however low we set it – we all end up falling short of it. So we can shake our heads angrily over some news item about an individual found guilty of fraud and then, without a second thought, set about creatively modifying our own tax returns. Or we can criticise a colleague's intolerance while neglecting the fact that we are constantly criticising our own neighbours. Ultimately, all human beings are hypocrites. In fact, you could argue that the most subtle form of hypocrisy is to see it as a problem you don't have.

Is the church full of hypocrites? That, I suggest, depends on your definition. The church is certainly full of those who have realised that they fall short of God's standards, and that's the way it ought to be. Jesus was known as 'the friend of sinners' and two thousand years later he keeps that title.

Let me end, however, by mentioning something that must not be overlooked. In the nature of things, those people, whether religious leaders or not, who talk about what is right and wrong put themselves in the spotlight and are inviting to be scrutinised for hypocrisy. Yet the one religious leader who has never attracted the charge of being a hypocrite is Jesus of Nazareth. Given that he set the highest morality the human race has ever seen, this is something extraordinarily remarkable. It's worth remembering that to be a Christian is not to follow some fallible human teacher but Jesus. And take it from me, he will never let you down.

# ISN'T THE CHURCH JUST FULL OF GOOD PEOPLE?

There are many and varied objections that people can find to avoid attending Christian meetings. I've heard dozens: 'It's the only time of the week when we can be together as a family', 'I can't face another meeting in a busy week' and 'The music is too loud'. I'm not surprised at the number and range of these objections: I believe the devil has a good grasp of strategy and knows that it's far easier to crush Christians on a one-by-one basis than en masse in a church. Isolated sheep are easy prey for wolves.

The idea that church is full of 'good people' congratulating each other on how nice they are is actually pretty intimidating. Mark Twain once wrote of someone that 'he was a good man in the worst sense of the word' and the idea that the moment you enter the church doors someone is judging you is not appealing. Actually, in reality, no authentically Christian church should be full of those who claim the title 'good'.

So why then do Christians go to church? Let me suggest three reasons and each of them goes against what the church is sometimes accused of.

**FIRST,** Christians go to church not because they are good but because they are *sinners*. Any church that takes the Bible seriously should do two things: it should proclaim to people the bad news that they have fallen short of God's standards while *simultaneously* declaring the good news that there is forgiveness and grace through Jesus Christ. For Christians to go to church is to be reminded both of their wounds and how they can be healed; it is to be prompted about their debt but also to be told how they can have it repaid by the Son of God. Five hundred years ago the great reformer of the church Martin Luther pointed out that to be a Christian was to be, at the same time, both a sinner and righteous. Because our rebellion against God has blurred our sense of right and wrong, we need to be constantly reminded from God's Word and through his Holy Spirit of how we should be living in the world. If a church is doing its job properly no one there should be proud of their morality or their spiritual achievements; there should, though, be a universal awareness of the need for God's grace.

**SECOND,** Christians go to church not because they know everything but because they are *students*. The 'bad news' of the gospel is not simply that our lives are a mess, it is that our thinking is a mess as well. We have all spent far too long listening to lies in every area of life. We have absorbed the frequently false values of the world from television, from advertisements, from the Internet and from those thousands of unremarkable, ordinary conversations we have with family, friends and colleagues. Every day in

147

countless different ways we are told, whether in shouted voices or through quiet whispers, what we are to believe and what we are to do. Those values inevitably affect – or infect – who we think we are and who and what we want to be. To become a Christian is to commit to learning God's truth, to making it a priority in our lives and to applying it to all that we are.

THIRD, Christians go to church not because they have won but because they are *soldiers*. Although it may come as an unwelcome truth, the fact is that anyone who puts their faith in Christ will find themselves engaged in a lifelong and unceasing battle against spiritual forces who want them to surrender. Every day, whether through subtle or direct attacks, Christians are faced with the temptation to fall short of being who they are meant to be. As in every conflict, there is strength in numbers and church is where we gather our forces together. Together, we become a fellowship where there is the binding of spiritual and psychological wounds, encouragement for those who are faltering and protection for one another with care and prayer.

So Christians go to church not because they are good but, on the contrary, they go because they need help.

I am reminded of Jesus' parable of the Pharisee and tax collector (Luke 18:9–14) where a self-righteous religious individual, proud of his own achievements and well aware of the sins of others, leaves the temple without being made right with God. In contrast, the unpopular tax collector, guilty of many sins, simply seeks God's mercy and leaves having been made right with God.

The great challenge for churches everywhere is to boldly set out the standards of good and right while at the same time holding out forgiveness for those who need it. It's not an easy balance but it's one we have to try to keep.

# IF JESUS IS GOING TO COME BACK SOON WHY DO WE NEED TO LOOK AFTER THE PLANET?

Let me start by saying that, along with Christians of every age, I firmly believe in the Second Coming of Christ: that one day the created world will be transformed and renewed by the return of God the Son back into the visible universe. I don't know when, or how, it will happen, but I know that it will be a moment of unimaginable awesomeness. The Second Coming will be a sudden, unexpected and unstoppable interruption of our daily lives by God himself and it will mark the end of history as humanity has known it.

That said, I am cautious about the Second Coming being used in an argument like this. One reason is that we have had nearly two thousand years of people predicting that Christ will come in the next few days or years and so far the failure rate is *precisely* one hundred per cent. We are in fact specifically warned by Jesus that the Second Coming will be at a time unknown to anybody (Matthew 24:36–44; 1 Thessalonians 5:1–3; 2 Peter 3:10; Revelation 3:3). The return of Christ may not even be imminent. There are hints in the New Testament that Jesus himself believed his return might only be after a considerable period of time; at least three of our Lord's parables suggest a long delay (Matthew 24:48; 25:5; 25:19). Yes, we should be prepared for the Second Coming to occur at any moment, but we must also accept that may still be centuries away.

A second reason is that we never apply the idea that the Second Coming is imminent to anything else. Does anybody seriously suggest that their children don't need to be educated because Christ is going to come back soon? Abandon the idea of marriage because of the impending end of all things? I think not.

But why do we need to look after the planet? There is really only one reason why we shouldn't neglect nature and it's a practical one: if we don't care for the earth, the human race will pay the price.

Let me give you four good Christian reasons for looking after the natural world.

FIRST, *to neglect nature is to show disrespect to God.* What we see in nature is God's handiwork and as such it reflects his wisdom, majesty and power. Could we but see it, every plant, animal and landscape has God's signature on it and how much we respect nature shows how much we respect him. After all, if some brilliant artist gave you a great painting you would look after it carefully and do your utmost to avoid any damage to it. Some theologians would even go further: they would argue that the universe in all its splendour and grandeur is in fact the temple of God. If so, then to damage creation is to vandalise God's temple – the most serious act of disrespect imaginable. However we view the natural world, we should show it care and respect. After all, one day we will meet the One who made it.

SECOND, *to neglect nature is to deny our role as God's stewards.* At the very beginning of the Bible God gives human beings orders to look after the created world (Genesis 1:28; 2:15). Despite our rebellion against God, nowhere in the Bible do we see those orders to rule and care for the world removed. The way that God governs his creation with love and faithfulness (see, for example, Psalm 104) is a model of how we are to rule the natural world. We should seek to be good and wise stewards of what has been entrusted to us.

THIRD, *to neglect nature is to risk God's displeasure.* If you have ever lived in rented accommodation you were probably subject to one of those end-of-tenancy inspections in which a landlord went through the lodgings ticking off on a clipboard what property was present, damaged or absent. It is no great stretch of the imagination to think that something very similar may occur at the Second Coming and, if so, I'm afraid there's going to be quite a bit of discomfort at the sheer quantity of animals and plants that are absent because we have let them become extinct. I wonder what this landlord is going to say about what we have done to his rainforests or the Great Barrier Reef. There's a very uncomfortable verse in the book of Revelation about God 'destroying those who destroy the earth' (Revelation 11:18).

**FOURTH**, *to neglect nature is to ignore our responsibility to others.* One of the most basic Christian rules is that we are to love our neighbour. The unfortunate fact is that most of the people affected by environmental problems are the world's poor who cannot buy their way out of trouble by moving elsewhere. Our neglect of the natural world hurts the weakest. We must also think not just of our responsibilities to the living, but also to those not yet born. The destruction we are allowing to occur to so much of the natural world will inevitably reduce the quality of the lives of future generations. The fact that our children and grandchildren may live on an impoverished and polluted planet, knowing only such things as a rhinoceros or a polar bear as zoo animals or screen images, is because of us. I'm afraid to say that we are guilty of theft from future generations.

# IF GOD IS TOTALLY IN CHARGE, WHAT'S THE POINT OF PRAYING?

This is another question that raises interesting challenges. Let me highlight them by rephrasing and expanding the question like this: 'If God is all-knowing and all-powerful and can do what he pleases, why does he want us to ask him for things?' It's a fair point. After all, supposing I need a new job, why should I bother praying about it? God knows better than me exactly what I need and he can fix it without my help. And just to complicate matters we could also add that if God knows the future then he already knows whether or not I'm going to get this job. It's also a question with an interesting flipside: if we fail to pray, do we hinder God's purposes? Does God ever sigh sadly about some new venture or possibility, 'A pity I can't do this because no one has prayed for it'?

Before I try and give some answers, it's important to point out that the focus of this question isn't ideal because it makes us think that prayer is all about *getting* and *achieving*. That's a viewpoint which encourages us to think of prayer as being some sort of cause-and-effect process in which God becomes little more than a cosmic vending machine: you decide what you want, insert the appropriate prayer and out comes the result. Now of course there is a strong element in prayer about asking and receiving: think of what Jesus teaches in the gospels (Matthew 6:11; 9:38; John 14:13–14) and Paul writes in his letters (Ephesians 6:19; Colossians 4:3–4; 2 Thessalonians 3:1–2). Nevertheless, while getting answers is part of prayer, it's not everything that prayer is about. In fact, only one very short clause in the Lord's Prayer ('give us today our daily bread', Matthew 6:9–13) is about asking for anything.

An old guideline for prayer was to think of it as something that went progressively through ACTS: *Adoration*, *Confession*, *Thanksgiving* and only then *Supplication* (a now little-used word for asking for things). It reminds us that making requests should only be part – and possibly the last part – of what praying is about. Indeed, someone has said that even if God never answered our prayers, he would still be someone worthy of our praise, confession and thanks. Nevertheless, if we like to think of God as being our heavenly parent, you would expect him to answer our prayers. And he does!

So actually, much of praying shouldn't really raise questions about how God's actions and our prayers interact. Nevertheless, some praying does and, as we grapple with this question, we find ourselves having to deal with such problem issues as free will and whether or not God knows the future. Precisely because it involves these things, 'Why should we pray?' is not an easy question to answer. Let me offer you some thoughts that may be helpful.

**FIRST**, *praying is something we are commanded to do.* Think of a real-world situation where a small child is about to pick up a dirty bottle from the ground with the clear intention of chewing on it. At this point the sensible parent doesn't give the child a lecture on bacteria and their perils but instead snaps out the command, 'Put that down immediately!' This principle can be extrapolated to God who is our heavenly Father: there are times when he tells us to do things without giving us an explanation. Prayer is one of them. Throughout the Bible we are told to pray, and I don't think we are told anywhere *why* we should pray. It's an order and whether we understand it or not we would be wise to obey.

**SECOND**, *praying does change things.* It's a fascinating if slightly embarrassing fact that for all their many achievements, scientists are not entirely sure about why cyclists do not fall off their bicycles. That failure to understand what's going on when you pedal does not stop millions of people every day cycling to work. (Indeed, one guaranteed way of falling off your bike is to worry about why you aren't falling off it!)

The reality of life is that we trust lots of things whose innermost workings we don't understand: in my case, that includes aeroplanes, smartphones and microwave ovens. And the fact is that whether we understand it or not, prayer works. This is what the Bible teaches us (see Genesis 18:16–33 and 2 Kings 20:1–11). Moses prayed for water and food for the Israelites (Exodus 15:24–25; Numbers 11:4–34) and Elijah asked God for fire from heaven (1 Kings 18:36–38). James tells us we don't get good things because we don't pray and also that the prayer of a righteous person accomplishes much (James 4:2; 5:16). Life confirms this biblical wisdom. I have known countless cases when I have seen remarkable answers to prayer. It works. The Bible does not tell us how prayer works and indeed it is perfectly likely that this side of heaven (where I assume we get some sort of mental upgrade) it may not be possible to know how it does works. But that shouldn't worry us: let's pray.

THIRD, *praying builds our relationship with God*. Another way of looking at prayer is not to focus on what it achieves in terms of actual observable effects but on what it produces in us. Prayer bonds us to God in several ways.

- Prayer reminds us of our dependence on God. To pray is to admit that God our Father is in control and that everything good comes from him (see Luke 11:11–13). Prayer undercuts any belief we might have that we are in charge of our lives.

- Prayer puts us on the same side as God. To pray is to seek to find God's will and bend our will to his. You can think of prayer as being like joining up with some demonstration of solidarity; it is to say to God, 'I am committed to who you are and what you are doing; I stand alongside you.' Prayer builds our relationship with God. When we pray we are not twisting the arm of God, but holding the hand of God.

- Prayer involves us in God's purposes. Think, for
  instance, of a parent inviting their child into the kitchen
  as they make a cake. 'You can help me,' the parent says
  and of course often the actual aid the child gives is
  minimal, but that isn't the point. The child's action
  involves them with what the parent is doing; when the
  cake comes out of the oven, they can say it is 'my cake'.
  Prayer serves the same function with our heavenly
  Father. God is a team player: he wants us to be involved
  with him through prayer.

Incidentally, the fact that prayer is about more than getting
results helps explain why some prayers go unanswered. God
as our heavenly Father retains the right of veto over our
prayers; we may not get that promotion or that sports car,
not because our prayers were inadequate, but simply because
God knows that it wouldn't be good for us.

Now you may not find these answers very satisfactory. The
fact of the matter is that there is a mystery associated with
prayer; a mystery that, this side of heaven, we will never
understand. The key point, however, is not to worry about
the theory, but continue with the practice. *Pray!*

# WHEN DOES LIFE BEGIN?

While most of the questions here are about puzzling issues that do not greatly impact on how we live, this one does: it is a life-or-death matter and one that many people find deeply troubling. For another, defining the beginning (or the end) of life is not easy. The fact is that although the moment of conception and the moment of birth are distinct events, everything else in between is some sort of continuous process.

Precisely because it is a process, the point at which life begins is debated. Some people say life begins when the egg is fertilised, and certainly from the genetic point of view that's when a new organism comes into being. Others would say it's when the egg is implanted just a few days later, while still others would argue that a foetus becomes alive after a few weeks when there is something detectable as a heartbeat. Still others would point to something like the tenth or twelfth weeks of development when there is a clear human shape, most organs have formed and there are detectable brainwaves. Certainly, by weeks twenty to twenty-four what we are dealing with is no longer a foetus but a baby and indeed babies are increasingly born alive from week twenty-one. The fact that from this stage in development babies can be born and live is recognised by the fact that almost all countries that allow any termination of pregnancy cease to allow it beyond this point, except if the mother's life is at risk. And while you might assume that everybody would count the moment of birth as marking the arrival of a living human being, certain philosophers exist who say that all new-borns should be subject to 'quality control' before being granted human status and allowed to live. So there's a great range of views and on medical grounds alone it's difficult to make a choice, although it's significant that very few people would deny the unborn infant 'human status' beyond week twenty-four.

The Bible clearly states that life begins at conception. Consider, for example, Psalm 139:13–16:

> 'For you created my inmost being; you knit me together in my mother's womb. I praise you because I am fearfully and wonderfully made; your works are wonderful, I know that full well. My frame was not hidden from you when I was made in the secret place, when I was woven together in the depths of the earth. Your eyes saw my unformed body; all the days ordained for me were written in your book before one of them came to be.'

There are Bible verses which talk about God's involvement in a life before birth. For example, 'Before I formed you in the womb I knew you, before you were born I set you apart;

I appointed you as a prophet to the nations' (Jeremiah 1:5) and, 'Before I was born the Lord called me; from my mother's womb he has spoken my name' (Isaiah 49:1). Job 31:15 and Isaiah 44:24 also tells us that there is no fundamental difference in status between the baby still in the womb and the baby when it is outside the womb.

That the unborn baby has some sort of spiritual status is suggested in Luke 1:41 where John the Baptist in Elizabeth's womb leaps in the presence of the unborn Jesus. Also significant are those passages which prophesy about how Mary will be able to give birth to Jesus (Matthew 1:18–25; Luke 1:26–38), telling us that God will intervene miraculously through the power of the Holy Spirit to allow conception. To me this says that, even in the womb, Jesus was always the Son of God.

I believe human life begins at conception and despite what our culture would tell us, what is in the womb is of great value. We need to care for unborn infants, not find ways of getting rid of them.

# ISN'T JESUS JUST AN IMAGINARY FRIEND?

Keeping going in the Christian life involves wrestling with issues and battling challenges to belief. This particular attack on the Christian faith is a popular one. The argument goes that our belief – particularly our faith in Jesus – is simply a grown-up version of the fantasy, common to many children, of having an imaginary friend with whom they hold conversations.

On this basis, the allegation is that our prayer and worship is no more than us conversing with some fantasy Jesus; we are, in effect, talking to ourselves. Those who wish to attack Christianity find it an attractive challenge because it carries both the scornful implication that Christians are childish and the affirmation that they, in contrast, are grown-up

men and women who don't need a psychological prop. Indeed, it's the sort of argument that is normally expressed in a sneering tone.

Let's consider it carefully as an argument. There are two aspects to this notion of an 'imaginary friend'. The first is that the Christian idea that a real, but invisible, Jesus exists and listens to what we say to him is nothing more than a total fantasy. The second is that this imaginary figure is a *friend*, a 'mate' or a 'buddy'; some cosy, affirming figure who comforts us in difficult times, makes us feel loved and who, in constant support, walks alongside us through life's challenges.

**WITH REGARD TO THE FIRST ELEMENT,** the reality is that the evidence for a Jesus who is not simply a figure of the past but someone who is alive today and willing and able to receive our prayers is substantial. One of the remarkable features of the Jewish faith is that it kept a great and unbridgeable gap between human beings and God; yet something about Jesus of Nazareth persuaded many Jewish people, including his closest followers, that, in him, God was physically present on earth. The gospels speak of a figure whose words claimed and deeds demonstrated that he was much more than a man. In the 2,000 years since his coming to earth, the Christian church has confidently declared that Jesus is alive, that he can be worshipped and that we can have a relationship with him. To say he is such a real and trustable figure is indeed an act of faith; but to deny it is also an act of faith.

THE SECOND ELEMENT, that this 'imaginary figure' exists because we need to be comforted by an illusory friend, is by no means as convincing as it sounds. I think there are two arguments against it: psychological and practical.

The *psychological* argument against Jesus being an imaginary friend is easily made. In any sizeable church you would find an extraordinary range of individuals: extroverts, introverts, optimists and pessimists; some would have had happy childhoods, some unhappy; some would have become Christians as children and some as adults. Nevertheless, all would claim to have a personal relationship with God through Jesus. The very diversity of people and their experiences makes the idea that this is some sort of psychological disorder or lingering childhood fantasy unlikely.

The second *practical* argument against Jesus being an imaginary friend centres on the nature of friendship because friends can be divided into what you might call 'soft' and 'tough' categories, and these are very different. A 'soft' friend will let you do whatever you want to do, even if it's unwise or wrong and will tell you what you want to hear. In contrast, a *'tough'* friend, although generally supportive, may disagree with what you're doing and will always try to guide you into doing what is good or right even if you don't want to do it. The Bible's use of the word 'friend' is that of a 'tough' friend; someone who has such a close commitment to your well-being that they will always be honest with you. In the New Testament Jesus was known as the friend of sinners (Luke 7:34; 15:2) and told his disciples they were his friends (John 15:15). The seriousness of that friendship was demonstrated by Jesus promising that he would lay down his life for his friends (John 15:13). That importance is echoed by his definition of our commitment to him: 'You are my friends if you do what I command' (John 15:14). In the Bible the idea that Jesus is our friend is matched by the idea that Jesus is our Lord.

For many Christians (and I would want to include myself here), the friendship that exists between us and Jesus is a 'tough' friendship. It is not simply a relationship that comforts, consoles and affirms but one that challenges, guides and rebukes. For most Christians, communicating with God or Jesus in prayer can, at times, be distinctly uncomfortable. We often find ourselves reminded of things that we should have done but haven't and things that we have done that we most definitely shouldn't have. We often, too, find in our praying that we are given challenges or even orders that naturally speaking we would prefer not to have. So, for example, we may be told to take up some task, to visit a difficult person or to show kindness to someone we would rather not. Indeed, I know people whose friendship with Jesus has cost them their jobs, the opportunity of getting married and, in some cases, losing their lives. (Somehow, I can't imagine any Roman philosopher sitting in the amphitheatre watching faithful Christians getting gutted by gladiators or becoming lunch for lions coming up with the idea that the victims believed in Jesus because it was a comfortable idea.) This sense of dealing with no-nonsense Jesus who doesn't take orders from us, doesn't fit at all with any sort of self-affirming, comfortable buddy that the imaginary friend argument requires.

So psychologically and practically, I think the idea that the Jesus we believe in is an imaginary friend is an argument that lacks any strength. Perhaps, however, it is best challenged not by counter-arguments but in the theatre of life. The idea that Jesus is real rather than imaginary is best underpinned not by historians and archaeologists or philosophers but by those ordinary believers who have such a living, vital relationship with him that they have been changed into very different people. In the book of Acts we read how the early Christians were recognised as being distinctively different from those around them and the reason given for the difference was that they had 'been with Jesus' (Acts 4:13). And I can testify to that personally today.

# SHOULD I GIVE MONEY TO BEGGARS ON THE STREETS?

It's very easy to focus our moral outrage on people engaged in dramatic crimes far away. It's easier to focus on the moral challenges that we don't face, than on the ones we do.

One particular challenge that many of us face on a regular basis comes when we encounter those who try to beg from us on streets or trains. This is not a trivial question. After all, in some places those who beg are so numerous that if you loaded up your pockets with change, they'd be empty in a matter of minutes. It also raises complex questions. Is this the wisest way to give money? Are we simply encouraging more begging? Are we in fact helping those who are truly needy? Equally, by giving are we treating genuine poverty or are we fuelling a drug or alcohol habit, or even subsidising laziness? Or are we actually being conned and this is a well-orchestrated crime racket? It's not an easy subject and I know that many of us struggle with it.

I would suggest that, in fact, there are a number of things that we should give to such people and money is only one of them. Indeed, money may not be the most important thing we can give the needy on the streets.

FIRST, we should give such people *our compassion.* To show compassion is more than simply offering charity, it is to have an attitude of genuine sympathy, kindness and respect. Perhaps, above all, it allows us to relate to individuals as people, rather than problems. In fact, personally I would prefer to avoid using the word 'beggar' which is a label that seems to dehumanise and diminish those who are on the street; the reality is that what we face are fellow human beings who are seeking help. An extreme lack of compassion can be seen in those who declare that they want to solve 'the problem of beggars' not because they care for them as individuals but because they want 'to clean up the town'.

As Christians we believe that *every* human being, even those who are dirty and unwashed, are made in the image of God and as such have an infinite value. So, when you come across someone begging please don't ignore them: acknowledge they exist, look at them and if you can't or choose not to give them money, give them some food. At the very least refuse their request politely.

If someone is begging in an area that you regularly cross and you meet them more than once, then talk to them, learn their name and greet them by it as you pass by. It's actually a great act of kindness to sit and talk to such people. You will surely help them to feel valued and you may even find out that there is a practical way that you can be of assistance, such as connecting them with a charity which can help them. In fact, it's worth remembering that it's easy to display a cold, compassionless charity and while our money may be welcomed by those who receive it, I'm sure the attitude isn't.

**SECOND**, we should give those 'on the streets' *our comprehension*. Homelessness and begging don't just happen; there is always a reason or reasons why people find themselves in this situation. One of the classic problems with homelessness is of well-meaning people who leap in offering insensitive solutions that ignore the needs of individuals in a particular area. Try to understand what's happened. Let me suggest three questions to ask about those who are begging, either from those who know them or from the individuals themselves.

- *Who are they?* What are their stories? How have they got into the state they are in?

- *What are their needs?* Things may not be as simple as they seem. Many individuals on the street seem to prefer the freedom of homelessness to the constraints of being in some sort of managed hostel. Do they just need money or do they need more, or different, help? If they do want money, what is it for? If it's for food, and you have the time, offer to buy them something. Of course, if it is obvious that what they want is alcohol, then to offer money may actually be doing more harm than good. And those on the street may want more than money; on a cold winter's night blankets and warm clothing are always very welcome.

- *What's being done for them?* Many churches or other organisations do things like 'soup runs' and it's no bad thing to take part on at least a fact-finding basis. Make enquiries about what is being done for them. What resources, such as soup kitchens and night refuges, already exist?

To give such people comprehension helps us to get alongside them. It also enables us to speak with some authority and experience about the problem. Perhaps, above all, it keeps us humble and grateful before God. Anyone who has listened to the stories of people who are on the street will end up uttering that wise phrase: 'There but for the grace of God, go I.'

FINALLY, we should give such people *our commitment.* One of the problems with us handing out cash is that it gives us the illusion of solving a problem. The reality is that we are not solving the problem, we are merely treating a symptom of it. We should make a commitment to those who are at the bottom of the social pile that is deeper, wider and more long-term than some thrown coin. We need to target the roots of the problem rather than its fruits. The big challenge with begging and homelessness is preventing getting people into that situation in the first place and, if they are already on the street, then getting them off it, not just for a day or a night but for life. By all means give but far better in my view than spare change is regular and systematic contributions to some organisation that you know is working effectively in this area. If you belong to a church, encourage it to support any work with the homeless. If all else fails, contribute to the Salvation Army whose expertise and success in working with the homeless is beyond challenge. Another thing we can do is make sure that dealing wisely and kindly with the homeless and rough sleepers is high on the agenda of our local council. There's a nasty tradition of trying to solve the problem of homelessness by merely moving individuals on to the next town. We need to ensure that everybody is aware that the word 'homeless' should never mean 'worthless'.

Should we give money to those who are begging? I would suggest that there is no simple answer to that. But what I am sure of is that we should give such people compassion, comprehension and commitment.

# DOES GOD CARE ABOUT ME?

In a sense this is one of the most important questions that we have raised so far. Certainly, if you are not yet a Christian but believe that God exists, it is probably something that you're concerned about. Actually, it's a question in two parts: firstly, does God *care*? Secondly, does he care *for me*?

The caring bit about God is very important. You see, it's relatively easy to believe in a God who is all-powerful, all-knowing and all-wise: a wonderful being so great and glorious that he can make a giraffe and manage a galaxy. Yet such a God could exist but be a cold and impersonal being: the Universe's Chief Executive, far too preoccupied to care for us.

The Bible's picture of God is very different and it repeatedly refers to him as someone who cares and indeed loves all he has made. In the Old Testament one of the great definitions of God is found in Exodus 34:6–7 where we read that God 'passed in front of Moses, proclaiming, "The LORD, the LORD, the compassionate and gracious God, slow to anger, abounding in love and faithfulness, maintaining love to thousands, and forgiving wickedness, rebellion and sin."'

When we read the long history of the Old Testament, we see an enormous amount of evidence that God cares. He makes covenants with people, answers prayer and rescues individuals (and nations) from disaster. The stories of the Old Testament are full of individuals such as Moses, Joshua, Ruth, David and Esther, and they tell us how God dealt personally with them. That language of care and covenant love used in the Old Testament becomes stronger and richer in the New Testament where we read repeatedly of God's love to men and women.

Yet in the New Testament we see these great Old Testament expressions of God's love suddenly change into something dramatically different and infinitely richer. God's care now goes beyond offering words, actions and faint glimpses of himself to a dramatic, personal intervention. Extraordinarily, beyond all comprehension, God himself comes to us as a human being – Jesus of Nazareth – and if that were not enough, goes to the cross and suffers there. The life and death of Jesus means many things but one thing it declares loudly is that God loves us to an extraordinary degree. It is as if God looks at the tragic, turbulent mess that is this world, recognises that no amount of religious teaching is going to save it and instead steps in to intervene personally. The cross proclaims that God loves each one of us enough to die for us.

OK, God cares, but you may have a reservation: does he care for *me* personally? After all, you might say, what reason is there for this great God to be particularly bothered about little me? I am an ordinary person, with ordinary concerns, in a world of around eight billion people.

I understand the concern but let me turn this on its head for you with a question. Why wouldn't God be concerned for you? The Bible teaches how God reached out to all sorts of people, from all sorts of backgrounds. Indeed, if there is any bias in who God accepts, it seems to be towards the weak, the insignificant, the ordinary and the unlikely. Jesus pointed out that it was those who knew they were sinful who responded better to him than those who thought they were good. God welcomes all who turn to him in repentance, trusting in the death and resurrection of Jesus Christ to save them. No one is too insignificant or too bad for God.

If you want further reassurance, just look at the two thousand years of Christian history. It's full of stories of individuals who, having recognised that their lives were a mess and heard that Jesus Christ offered them a new life, have turned to him and had all that they were completely transformed.

Does God care for you? Yes, he does. There's a verse in a psalm that is, in effect, an offer from God: 'Taste and see that the Lord is good; blessed is the one who takes refuge in him' (Psalm 34:8). Does God care for you? Yes, he does and I encourage you to *receive him* and *know him.*

# ON QUESTIONS AND QUESTIONING

Looking back, I see that we have covered an enormous and varied amount of material. I hope that if you have been considering the Christian faith and have had specific questions that were troubling you that I've been able to help answer them. And even if your specific question was not answered I trust you've arrived at this page with the sense that whatever your question is, it probably *could* be answered. I'm not convinced that people can be entirely argued into the Christian faith but I am confident that the objections to Christianity can be answered.

In closing let me address two groups of people: those who are believers in Christ and those who are, for the moment at least, outside Christianity.

FIRST, and briefly, to 'believers'. I hope that some of these answers have been helpful to you. Even if they haven't answered the particular questions that may be troubling you, I hope they have shown you that Christian faith can be defended and that they may have pointed you to ways in which you could answer both your own questions and others. Do remember, however, that being a Christian is not about having your questions answered but about living your life with Jesus and for Jesus. Indeed, I suspect that there are many Christians who walk around with unanswered questions stacked away somewhere in their minds, quietly confident that the day will come when the Lord of all will give them answers. Christianity is not a philosophy that must be completely thought out; it is a relationship to be lived out.

If you found a group of people who had become Christians and asked them what had drawn them into making a commitment, I suspect that very few of them would say that they had been argued into it. Far more, I imagine, would say it was something about how Christians lived that drew them to the faith. A well lived out faith without all the answers to life's questions is better than a poor faith with all the answers.

SECONDLY, let me make some comments to those of you who are still enquiring about Christianity. I hope I have answered at least some of your questions and, if I haven't answered all of them, that at least I have persuaded you of the possibility that your questions could be answered.

Nevertheless, having praised questioning so far, let me now point out that there are risks with it. You're probably well aware of what psychologists call a 'displacement activity': the way that when we are faced with a difficult decision we are suddenly able to find something else that needs doing, whether it be making a coffee, changing the printer cartridge or even doing the ironing. In my experience it's all too common to find that when someone is investigating the Christian faith there comes a point where they continue to ask questions, not because they are gripped by serious intellectual issues but because questions are a way of postponing making a decision for Christ.

Indeed, if you are on the way to becoming a follower of Jesus, let me ask you a question: if I was to answer all your questions would you become a Christian? The fact of the matter is that to become a Christian is not simply to agree to some view of how the world works but to put yourself under the lordship of Christ. If you choose to believe in Jesus then there are implications for how you live. Changed beliefs must result in changed lives; faith must produce works.

Thinking about questions reminds me that in the New Testament there are at least three occasions where Jesus is asked a question but his response is not simply to give an answer.

Consider Luke 13:23–24 where someone asked Jesus, 'Lord, are only a few people going to be saved?' Jesus' reply was simply,

'Make every effort to enter through the narrow door, because many, I tell you, will try to enter and will not be able to.'

There's another case, at the very end of John's gospel, where Peter asks Jesus about the destiny of another disciple, probably John. 'When Peter saw him, he asked, "Lord, what about him?" Jesus answered, "If I want him to remain alive until I return, what is that to you? You must follow me"' (John 21:21–22).

Let me give you another illustration. In the book of Acts we read that just outside Jerusalem the disciples gathered around the resurrected Jesus 'and asked him, "Lord, are you at this time going to restore the kingdom to Israel?" He said to them: "It is not for you to know the times or dates the Father has set by his own authority. But you will receive power when the Holy Spirit comes on you; and you will be my witnesses in Jerusalem, and in all Judea and Samaria, and to the ends of the earth"' (Acts 1:6–8).

Did you notice that in all three cases Jesus not only refuses to answer the question but instead gives a command? 'Enter the kingdom yourself', 'Follow me', 'Be my witnesses.' Questioning has its limits. Ultimately there comes a point where we simply have to decide: do I follow Jesus? What's your answer?

That's the real question. This time, however, the answer is up to you.

# THAT'S A GOOD QUESTION!

**Who made God? Where is heaven? Does God sleep?
Were there dinosaurs on the ark?**

Questions are so important – they are how we learn
to live our lives. *That's a Good Question!* is a collection
of 32 questions commonly asked by children, which
J.John answers in a clear, concise and compelling way.
The book is complemented by creative appealing illustrations.

Order online at **www.canonjjohn.com**.

# JESUS CHRIST – THE TRUTH

There is no denying the importance of Jesus Christ
in the history of humankind.

In *Jesus Christ – The Truth*, J.John and Chris Walley
achieve an uncommon blend: a serious book for
popular use and a popular book for serious reading.

If you want to know who Jesus Christ is, then read this book.

Order online at **www.canonjjohn.com**.

'I've asked almost all of these questions myself
over the course of my life and am so grateful that
my friend J.John has compiled and answered them together
in one volume. *Will I Be Fat In Heaven?* is full of wisdom,
truth, insight, challenge, compassion and humour.'

### Christine Caine
Founder A21 and Propel Women


'This book is classic J.John – a cheeky title, searching
questions, and a deep passion to recommend the Christian faith
to any who are seeking. Whether you're cautiously pursuing
the claims of Christianity, or are already a follower of Christ,
this book has something to say to you. Brilliant!'

### Matt Redman
Worship Leader and Songwriter


'I am personally grateful for the faithful friendship of J.John
and his beautiful wife Killy. He has ministered across a number
of Hillsong campuses and has been a key speaker at our beloved
Colour Conference on several occasions. The way J.John has
framed and crafted this new book of pressing, poignant
and soul-defining questions will help multitudes discover
what they are looking for.'

### Bobbie Houston
Co-Global Senior Pastor, Hillsong Church


'This book is J.John at his best. Clear, well-reasoned, honest
and compelling. He examines all the difficult questions we
might have about the Christian faith and with both kindness
and conviction gives thoughtful and helpful responses.
A must-read for thoughtful believers and genuine seekers.'

### Mike Pilavachi
Soul Survivor

'Have you been wrestling with questions for so long, but didn't know who to ask? Well my good friend J.John is here for you. With profound biblical understanding, empathy and humour he addresses the questions that many of us have had for years.'

**Sheila Walsh**

Singer and Broadcaster


'Believe me, there are people in your life who desperately need this book. It does what almost no books do, which is answer the real questions many people have about God, and which they yearn to have answered. I thank God that my friend J.John has used his obvious gifts at communicating in a way most of us can easily understand!'

**Eric Metaxas**

*New York Times* Bestselling Author of *Bonhoeffer* and *Is Atheism Dead?*


'Never in recent history has the entire planet been racked with so many questions about God, life, death, meaning, and purpose. J.John's book is a timely treasure trove of answers to humanity's quest for understanding. Whether you are wrestling with a question yourself or helping a friend in their spiritual journey, this book will help you navigate some of life's greatest questions.

**Carrie Boren Headington**

Adjunct Professor of Evangelism,
Fuller Theological Seminary

'The title alone made me want to read J.John's new book!
The fact is, in today's secular culture, few things could be
more powerful and effective than an entertaining,
well-written book about the "basics" of the Christian faith.
My great hope is that pastors start preaching from this book
because studies show the average church member is more
ignorant of these issues than we'd like to think.
Buy it today. I have a PhD in Theology
and I loved every minute reading it.'

**Phil Cooke, PhD**
Author of *Maximize Your Influence:*
*How To Make Digital Media Work For Your Church,*
*Your Ministry, and You.*


'J.John has his finger on the pulse of humanity.
He knows the questions they are asking
and he has answered them brilliantly.
He is a pristine voice in today's world of chaos and noise.'

**Yang Tuck Yoong**
Senior Pastor,
Cornerstone Community Church


'J.John has furnished us with a resource helping
everyone to reach out to people searching for answers.
Questions are the best starting point for deeper-level
conversations. This book will serve as a wonderful gift
for those we know are perplexed about some of
the mysteries of life. Great book.'

**Phil Pringle**
Leader, C3 Global

'The title of this book, *Will I Be Fat In Heaven?*, is an attention-grabbing question to invoke your curiosity, but in reality, this book is an in-depth biblical study on life's most important questions. If you have ever wondered about the afterlife – or why people suffer, or what is God really like, or why God allows evil, and of course what will your physical body look like in heaven – then this book by J.John is a must read.

### Pastor Dudley C. Rutherford
Shepherd Church,
Los Angeles, CA, USA


'J.John is one of the most gifted communicators of the Christian faith in the church today. He has a wonderful ability to present profound issues with clarity, wisdom and humour.'

### Nicky Gumbel
Vicar of Holy Trinity Brompton,
and Developer of the Alpha Course


'In this book J.John asks some of the questions that have rested on our lips and lie in our thoughts and consciousness about life as we know it and life beyond what we know.'

### Noel Robinson
Worship Leader


'This is an incredibly helpful starting point for those who want to make sense of the Christian faith and make sense of life, from one who has faithfully proclaimed and lived out its message over many years.'

### Rico Tice
*Christianity Explored*